She Breathes Infinity

Becoming a Body of Infinity

SHE BREATHES INFINITY
BECOMING A BODY OF INFINITY

BY

ELISE R. BRION

SHE BREATHES INFINITY: BECOMING A BODY OF INFINITY
COPYRIGHT © 2015 ELISE R. BRION

Published by Bliss-Parsons Institute, LLC
www.Bliss-Parsons.com
Editing, layout, and design by Susan Bingaman

All rights reserved. No part of this book may be reproduced or transmitted in any form or by any means without the written permission of the author and publisher.

The author of this book does not, either directly or indirectly, dispense medical advice, nor does she prescribe the use of any technique as a form of treatment for physical or medical problems without the advice of a physician. The intent of the author is to provide support and encouragement for your personal Spiritual and emotional development. Should you choose to apply any of the information in this book to yourself, as is your right, you do so at your own discretion. The author and publisher assume no responsibility for your actions.

ISBN: 978-0-9963-176-1-0

Library of Congress Control Number: 2015939392

DEDICATION

*This book is dedicated to
the One Lord God Almighty,
and to my Eternal, One and only Mother,
Who brought me forth into this existence by way of
Her Spirit in God Almighty, millions of years ago.*

Contents

Introduction
p. x

Suicide of the World: the Truth Unfolds
p. 1

The Battle Begins
p. 11

Negative Emotions Seen Through the Lens of the Holy Spirit
p. 15

From a Rock to a Pearl in God's Ocean of Healing
p. 21

The Look of the Healing:
God's Essence Through Nature
p. 29

Back to Weeks of Post Resurrection and More Nature Medicine
p. 41

The Rocky Healing Continues
p. 45

Trauma Leading to Triumph
p. 53

Famine of the Heart
p. 67

Regarding the Hatred of the Heart for
That Which is Pure
p. 73

God's Supernatural HUM and
My Early Years in This Lifetime
p. 81

A Prayer in Conviction of Christ's Healing Fire
p. 95

How Evil Attempted to Sever My Soul from Spirit
p. 97

Nurturing Good Amongst Evil
p. 111

Strike Three for the HUM
p. 113

A Second Dad
p. 117

The Teenage Years: Soul-Battles with the World
while Spirit Still Speaks
p. 121

The Fire of Infinity Breathes
p. 125

A Woman of God's Love and Two Women of the Qualities of the Divine Mother
p. 129

The Conclusion of Elise's Family Album
p. 135

Weaving God's Timeless Healing While Living In Earth Time
p. 137

On Becoming a Messenger of Infinity
p. 141

Anorexia or Soulful, Spiritual Cleansing?
p. 147

January 5, 2015: a Journal Entry
p. 157

On Confidence and Hope
p. 161

Becoming a Body of Infinity
p. 189

Faith as the Fire of the Living Body of Christ: Your Key to Becoming a Body of Infinity
p. 211

The Practical Application of Healing Principles
p. 215

Elise's Photo Album
p. 223

Introduction

This book radiates Christ's Healing in BECOMING A BODY OF INFINITY—not after your fleshly temple has passed, but right now. God's Divine Ocean of Indomitable Truth is awaiting your choice to Return unto it even while in body upon Earth, but the fullness of your being has become disconnected from this Truth. I have the power to Breathe Infinitely, so it is time to be Reborn.

I am made of God's boundless and Divine Truth. I am nothing without It, but made perfect in the communion of belonging to God—in the whole of who I really am. This supernatural Reality is the very substance and essence of all Life, and it is what now compels me to write this book that radiates the Purity of Christ's Healing Presence.

Humanity is in dire need of a complete spiritual and mental exorcism, a cleansing Ray so perfect that only the Truth of God's Healing Will is known. Mankind must **choose** this, and it will only be made manifest individual by individual. For this world has become a mica-thin globe of glass due to the evils that humanity has consciously brought forth for millions of years.

I write because there are many who are called, and the few who are chosen need this book's assistance so as to embody the Will of God in the cleansing and Healing of mankind. One more person who chooses thus will tip the scales in favor of the possibility of a future for the human species on Earth. To embody the Will of God is a grand task that few people on Earth fully understand, because it is a supernatural instruction.

Jesus so perfectly simplified it. The Holy Bible clearly states that a Child of God is to live in the Kingdom of Heaven, and He taught what it takes to live AS the Kingdom of Heaven. This has been forgotten by too many. It is God's Will that His Holy Kingdom be embodied NOW, not just when the flesh passes from this Earth.

What I share with you here is the very essence of what it takes in the journey of becoming a body of infinity, for I breathe and embody the Living Truth.

All Praise and Glory to the ONE Supernatural God Almighty!

My every breath, every atom, and every thought is born of raw devotion and timeless love for our God, Who Loves far greater than I, or anyone throughout the ages could ever possibly love. Even though I am upon this planet to emanate those aspects of God's Will which have been assigned to me for millions of years as the spirit being that I am, I have only just Returned to that Truth of who I am after years of suffering in this lifetime. Before coming into this lifetime on Earth, I had agreed to undertake a part of the journey of suffering as a means of assisting humanity towards the cleansing and Healing. God's Great Plan required it, and my spirit is ever Faithful. But my soul, which was formed exclusively within this world, took on far more than was necessary, and the suffering took on very dangerous degrees of evil.

This book is not just about my own Rebirth and Renewal in God's Body of Truth, it is a tutorial in embodying the Infinity of Life, here and now, for you.

***

My name is Elise R. Brion, and in this present moment, which is a continuous stream that goes beyond time and space, I claim the supernatural rays of God's Healing for you, in the Living Fire and NAME of Jesus the Christ. For I do not just believe, but I KNOW that God Almighty's ceaseless Body of Truth, Majesty, Indomitable Power, and Unconditional Love is ONE throughout all Life, making an impenetrable web of conviction that His Will of Healing is for all who would Receive. Come and taste of the Power of this Reality. Life is Divinely supernatural, and God's Will is for you to be Whole in His Way, His Truth, and His Life. My story directly assists you in rejecting that element of the world that is destruction, so as to embrace what IS the LIFE.

My book exposes the whole of who I have been in this lifetime, as Elise R. Brion, detailing the impossible Miracles made manifest through this body I use— Miracles brought forth exclusively by God Almighty, through His Son Jesus the Christ. More importantly, this book serves as a guideline for those who are devoted to being Healed in mind/body/heart/soul and who seek to live God's Infinity not upon the passing of the flesh, but NOW.

Let me be very clear here: What you will read is a revelation not just of one woman's intense mental, spiritual and physical Rebirth, but this autobiographical, hands-on testimony of God's Infinity will directly nourish and uplift each and every atom of your flesh, every wave of your mind, and the fullness of your spirit to His Healing Grace. How do I know this? I once was locked in to a worldly hell of evil disconnection and by way of God's Grace and with Jesus' Living Fire, I ROSE to destroy its shackles from the whole of my being. In this process of Awakening, I came to the eternal knowing that Pure Life is inseparable and unified, and Goodness is **exclusively from and of** our ONE God. Through Miraculous Healings, I was given a taste of the intrinsic communion of God's perfect web of life, and all beings, sentient and non-sentient, are a part of it. After all I have been through, I am committed to embodying and radiating the Healing Will of God Almighty, in the Name of Christ's Living WORD. I will it forth that this book will do what I say it will do for anyone who reads it.

I forewarn you that I am most unusual as judged by the gaze and opinion of the world at large, but truly, the few who are in full communion with God are indeed foreign to this world.

My life's story will not be shared in chronological order, but in the proper network by which I am guided to share it. Also, please note that contrary to "proper" English writing, I sometimes mix tenses in the same paragraph. Circumstances from my past may be commented on with a present tense expression. The future is always above and beyond the past and the present, and even though the human language is so poorly limited in properly depicting the REALITY that time exists only on Earth, I use English to the best of my ability, albeit a little non-conventionally. I am also known to "create" words, and if I use one that is not in the English dictionaries, you will clearly understand what is meant by it by way of my explanation.

The Healing from Christ requires retraining the mind to think beyond time, as His Healing is indeed timeless. This teaching is another supernatural part of this book's purpose. The whole of my story and the book's guideline to becoming a body of infinity will be clearer than the purest spring water, and I invite you now to drink deeply, giving attention to your own breath as you read.

Now, get ready for a washing of the Holy Spirit's Adoration for you in Healing, such as you have never experienced before. For no matter what you have been through or are presently enduring, Infinity cannot hold rays of suffering, and your birthright as the spirit being you are, is to Return unto Infinity NOW.

***

SUICIDE OF THE WORLD: THE TRUTH UNFOLDS

It was Good Friday in March of 1997.

My body was declared medically dead by suicide, deemed so by a team of EMTs who were called to the scene of my parents' garage, where a black Nissan Sentra was still running with the keys in the ignition. My flesh was gray and lifeless upon their arrival, with no heartbeat at 10:01 AM on that black Friday. Having dosed myself with a lethal amount of carbon monoxide from the engine's operation and the car set to park, they were not initially able to discern how long I had been dead, for the panic of the situation was high. But I had planned that suicide with a keen eye to the whole family's schedule for the day, what with my parents' assured absence due to work and travel. No one was home, and I was rock solid in focus upon the goal of departure from this world.

My mother had embarked upon a long drive out of the city for her work, but suddenly realized that she had forgotten some necessary keys to her office so she turned around and headed back to our hometown. To her great shock and horror, she discovered my lifeless body after the electric garage doors opened. Needless to say, she immediately rushed for the telephone to call 911.

The EMTs arrived within minutes, as the local hospital was less than two miles away. In that enclosed garage of a suburban house in west St. Louis County, Missouri, USA —one of the houses in which I had experienced my tumultuous childhood—my physical and worldly life, indeed, ended.

Three hours after the medically-declared death, God Almighty brought me back into the flesh, and here is what I experienced. But I must also share the facts of what occurred before I sat down silently in the car, as well as the Miraculous sight between that moment and the one in which I realized I had been brought back into this world, for that space of "time" is where Christ's Infinity Breathed, and I was taught how to inhale for the first time in this life.

You are experiencing a weaving of time in the retelling of my true stories as you watch this movie of my life. And yet we Praise God that His WORD is the Fire that burns ALL sufferings and transfigures a dead past unto His Living Will.

The curtain rises, and mind you, this is not a PG-rated film ...

I knew that my stepfather regularly took Coumadin because of his atrial fibrillation. Earlier that day I had consumed the whole bottle of his prescription medicine. I went to my childhood bedroom, with its Blue-Purple shag carpet and lavender walls and curled up in bed, hoping for a quick cessation of my heart's beating. Not understanding how the medication worked, I foolishly assumed that such a heavy dose of the blood thinner would shock my heart and stop it immediately. As nausea began to set in I headed for the bathroom and vomited, still feeling as if my intestines and heart were about to explode, but I was discontent with the thought that perhaps there was not enough drug in my flesh to end it. I turned on the bathtub faucet to run a bath, believing that drowning would be the next easiest choice. The nausea was making me delirious, as I sunk my head into the already-filled tub and told myself to breathe in the water very quickly.

Suicidal psychosis combined with fear is an evil beast, and as the internal physical pain was intensifying quickly, I could not handle the vision of my bloated and clothed body being discovered in the bathtub where I had played as a child. I saw flashbacks to happy moments—among them, myself as a very small toddler, throwing a rubber ducky at my older sister. The heart of my soul and greater still, my spirit, was fighting to grab hold of a diseased and seriously disconnected mind by way of these happy visions from my past. I could not bring myself to drown, and I somehow pulled myself out of the tub and crawled to my bedroom to change my clothes.

I had a set of keys to the spare car that was sitting in the garage, and I chose option number three for physical death. I needed death to be easy at this point, because suicidal thoughts are the most evil form of self-centeredness, and on top of that, I was in tremendous physical pain. I stumbled to the bathroom, ironically to take a cold drink of water from the faucet. As I took a look in the mirror I saw ugly horror and tremendous suffering, what with my face distorted and mangled-looking—an ashen ghost staring through the mirror. I did not even feel human. I was out of my mind. Taking a breath hurt bad at that point, and I rushed out of the bathroom in panic.

"Stop your breathing." This was the evil voice that had dominion in that moment, and I accepted it as my only solution. I chose to make it so by way of that car.

I decided that I wanted to float away painlessly, on the wavelengths of music. I truly believed that I could just leave this world as such, telling myself that music was just another form of energy, and wasn't my flesh just that? I knew from my spirit and by way of science studies that all matter was energy, light, and sound vibrations condensed into form. Being a musician and singer, who was polluted not only by lies of the mind but also by the liars of this world in the form of popular music, and being in a state of suicidal delirium, I put in Sinead O'Connor's CD, "I Do Not Want What I Haven't Got", and stumbled into the garage.

I kept the door from the garage to the house open for a few minutes, so that I could hear that horrible song, "Nothing Compares 2 U", as loudly as possible, before shutting the door to ensure that the garage would fill with as much carbon monoxide as possible. I turned the vehicle's engine on, and began to breathe as deeply as I could as tears streamed down my face. I was convinced that this was the end of a short and worthless lifetime of lies, deceit and psychological suffering. At 20 years of age, with a soul that had nearly disconnected from Christ, the last thing I remember was a famous quote from my then-favorite author, Kurt Vonnegut: And so on …

There was no darkened tunnel with a light at its end. There was an extremely fast, jumbled up vision of my tiny life's experiences that flashed within my consciousness, wherein I saw images of my fleeting joyous years when I was less than 8 years old, as well as the various scenes of tumult and despair during the short 12 years after. This flash-scroll was extremely quick and beyond time as humans experience it, but it was as real as the deadly chemicals destroying the cells of my body.

What came next was the beginning of my cleansing unto Infinity.

I was not in a body and I could see nothing, but the sense of the ENERGY of where I found myself was tremendous. Trillions upon trillions of tiny points of light were fused together and melding into each other. An awesome combination of crystal Whites, Golds, Rosy-Pinks, and an impossible to describe crystal Blue were shimmering all around me, and I was completely aware of being OF it, not separate from it. I was encapsulated in LOVE such as I had never experienced during this particular lifetime on Earth. I was inundated, saturated, held by this frequency, this BODY of LIGHT, and I did not want to leave that place. In that moment I could not name this energy as being "of God", but it was very clear to me that there was no separation between myself, and this holy energy in which I found myself existing within.

I began to "swim" around in this Body of Love, and as I did so, the trillions of light particles, (similar to a Pointillist painting of the Impressionist period) began to undulate, shifting with my every movement. Oh, for me it was heaven to dance in this way—in this supernatural, all-consuming radiant energy where I felt like I finally belonged. It was home, or my closest memory to home, that is.

Then a voice was made audible to me. It was a male-sounding voice that said, "You are not to stay here. You will return to my Plan. There are many who await you, and some whom you will bring to me."

Then the vision changed. Suddenly, I saw before me three young Children: a boy around 12 years of age, a girl slightly younger, and then a much smaller girl, around 1 or 2 years, all playing together in a grassy open field. An intense yearning for them began to fill me, and if there can be tears in the state I was in, I was certainly streaming my heart's passionate desire to hold them. It was revealed to me that these were my future Children. I wanted to run to them and scoop them up in my arms—to stay in that very place with them with Love I had forgotten in the life of the world in which I had entrenched myself. I burned to know them. I burned to give birth to them—those three blessed and beloved spirit Children.

I ached to have them stay with me, but then the scene changed, morphing into the last vision-scape.

I saw an oceanic horizon of people, mostly young Children and babies, positioned against the sky as if all of those people were the actual land, and their attention and focus was upon me. If my being could swell with passion any deeper than it had, upon viewing my own future Children, it was doing so in this dramatic moment.

The awesome realization of an Awakening within me was two-fold: The first and greater of the two was the realization that I was experiencing myself as my TRUE spirit, as the one whom I have been for millions of years. This state of joyous Love was one in which my most pure form found its resting place and familiarity. The second wonderful realization was in my tasting of the spiritual Agreement that I had made, over and over, throughout my existence AS a spirit being. What I am about to describe is part of that sacred covenant with God Almighty which I am; the very reason WHY I was given the name "Elise" for this lifetime, this body, and this soul's form—for the word "Elise" means "oath or covenant to God."

This part of my spiritual Agreement is to radiate my nature of and for divine Truth and Motherhood, to nourish and nurture all, so that the supernatural Reality of living in communion with God Almighty assists in the transfiguration of evil, into the Purity and Perfection of His Living and Divine WORD. In a world that has chosen terrible evils and disconnections as its normative way of existence, this particular Agreement has always been made manifest in my work within this world to teach and model Truth. In sum, I am of the Healing of God Almighty.

In that timelessness of being completely separated from my physical flesh, of being ALIVE in that space of crystalline brilliance, direction, and radiance of His Mercy, I was recharged by God Almighty back into the supernatural embrace that only He is, and that only He provides.

Everything was crystal clear to my spirit-mind, which is the only thing that existed. Nothing of my past had cognizance anymore in that timeless space of brilliance. Nothing of the world, nothing of my ego's entrapments, nor of the suffering (created by myself and the family I was born to) I had experienced even mattered. What mattered was this RECHARGE of clarity of my work for God's Life, this interfusion of Creator's Mercy within me, and the desire my spirit had to return to my body to see my spiritual tasks completed—my REAL work in this life.

However...

When I came back to consciousness in my flesh, I found myself in a hospital, inside a glass hyperbaric chamber, where 120% oxygen was being administered to my body.

And I was physically aware again. My conscious and subconscious minds were temporarily back in "control." My sin-ridden ego most certainly did NOT want to be back in the world. In fact, I was despondent at being there, feeling the weight of my evil-ridden subconscious and conscious mind. I did not have too long to dwell in such filthy despair, however, as I passed out into a deep sleep due to the trauma experienced by my body.

Now, hyperbaric chambers are risky business. Dosing out 120% oxygen could easily blow a physical body up and destroy the heart and/or brain, so the administration in the process must be carefully timed and monitored. I learned later from the medical team who treated me, of the intense science and leap of faith involved in its use because the level of carbon monoxide that had saturated my flesh was so high. With medical/scientific knowledge and brilliance, the whole team stayed the course with selflessness. (What blessed and beloved souls whom I will remember for Eternity!) They were "interfused", or consumed with the Hand of the Holy Spirit, and my body was successfully cleared of the poison, but my brain and heart had suffered tremendously.

And yet, after a two-day coma, with my body kept in ICU, I awoke.

I felt no physical pain, and had no memory of anything that had happened in the material world save for my last thoughts while sitting in the death car back at my parents' house. The nurses later told me that I had been declared brain dead, but there happened to be a single angelic doctor who absolutely insisted that my body be given a dose of charcoal to remove the destructive chemicals of the overdose of Coumadin, while being placed in the hyperbaric chamber. He was about to leave his shift that Good Friday of 1997 the moment my flesh was rushed into that hospital, and God placed him front and center in the workings of Christ's Healing so as to bring forth the impossible.

Three hours after my flesh was declared medically dead, my body started to show vital life readings, and 15 minutes later I came back into consciousness inside that glass womb of life-giving breath. *Praise God!*

The first thing I remember when I came to, was seeing my Father, Pacelli Escondo Brion, sitting right next to me holding my hand. He had a mixture of relief, sorrow, and joy upon his face, while he squeezed my hand tightly looking me straight in the eye, shaking.

I cracked a smile, but was not able to get any words out. I had suffered significant brain trauma and had a damaged heart due to oxygen deprivation. Coumadin is a blood thinner, and I had consumed a whole month's supply of this prescribed drug and it had remained in me for hours before my body was discovered. What with the damage I had done to myself, I would have been a vegetable for the rest of any life I was given, were it not for God's Awesome Mercy and Healing. *Bless GOD!*

But there I was, experiencing a different kind of hell on Earth. I was trapped inside a damaged body and a mind that was not functioning properly. For I could definitely think, albeit in a strictly emotional sort of consciousness, and I panicked about this, realizing that I was damaged internally, and further more, my own thoughts seemed to have no fluidity, no comprehensive quality ... even to myself.

I was cut off from making sense even to myself. But the one hellish thing that was kept absolutely perfect in spite of the deplorable state I was in, was my ability to feel despair, depression and sorrow. Ego's addictions were alive and strong, and it was my own "damned" fault. I use the word for its true meaning and not as a worldly expression.

***

The Battle Begins

In His Mercy and Righteousness, God Almighty had miraculously Saved my flesh, but He made me face the major work of CHOOSING to cleanse and Renew my own mind. He would continue to observe as to what degree my will would be directed, so as to Receive His Redemption and Salvation of heart, soul, and mind.

I would continue to grieve our Lord for a time, yet. This would be an uphill battle between my soul, my spirit, and a filth-ridden subconscious mind, whose stuffed pain and self-induced sorrows would lay deeply hidden, resurfacing for some years to come.

From a third person perspective, it stands to reason that after experiencing such a holy miracle, and after Receiving such a sacred Grace beyond the flesh only to be granted Life again, that one would have a burning desire to CHOOSE to progress in Healing. Knowing that what I had Received was indeed from God, it is a wonder that I did not instantly choose to repent and come back to Jesus the Christ as my personal Savior and the Savior of mankind. After all, I had been born, baptized, raised, and educated in a private Catholic school, attending a Catholic church and going to mass Monday through Friday before school and again on Sundays, for the whole of my Childhood. Why had this not been enough to carry me through the lies?

It seems only logical that after such a profound act of Love and Mercy from God, that my parents would have done everything in their power to see to it that their 20 year-old daughter was surrounded by Unconditional Love and tenderly nursed back into at least a functioning state of life. But this is a world of evil, filled with ignorance and disconnected from Truth. My parents were no exception to the rule; while I have fully Forgiven them in God's Unconditional Love, the facts must still be revealed.

First, I share the following about my father so as to honor his role in my eventual Rebirth into Truth, and to show you very clearly how ALL negative psychological conditions and emotions are NOT created by God. Humanity's belief that negative emotions are "just a part of human nature" is the biggest success of a defeated devil; for billions of people have barely survived life on this planet and have died defeated in soul and spirit because of this evil lie. In fact, if a soul dies without Returning to Christ, combined with choosing the hell of remaining consumed with emotional negativity at death, the probability of returning to one's true spiritual home in the cosmos is next to zero. For none are Saved but for the Grace of God.

My Filipino father, who had been diagnosed with congestive heart failure eight years prior to my suicide, was the one responsible for my tiny exposure to Truth in Christianity I received as a child. His aggressive insistence was the reason that I experienced 6 years of Catholic school education, attending Mass every day before school, and again on Sunday. Born in 1939 in the Philippine Islands, having come to America in the early 60s and then marrying my Caucasian, American-born mother, his own upbringing had led him toward two possible choices for his life: the priesthood or medicine. From an early age he showed unusual gifts of extrasensory perception, and he was the one that the family and the barrio community came to for soulful healing needs. My father decided that medicine was the path that God called him to, and as much as he loved the Philippines and his family, he came to America to live a renewed life distanced from the stories of war-torn sorrow of those Pacific Islands.

Sorrow and suffering carry forth through generations, staying lodged within the genetic blueprint of a bloodline, entrenched in the flesh, and most definitely manifesting in the character and behavior of present and future generations. My beloved father's stuffed rage regarding all the horrors that he witnessed growing up (including his own teenage brother being blown up by shrapnel), with both the Japanese and Americans often attacking the islands at the same time, combined with the varying personalities and egos of his family, as well as the conviction to live in American wealth and not the poverty of his childhood, made him a convoluted and complex individual. Mixed into his psyche was his strong Faith in the Righteousness of God Almighty, and devotional Catholic ways.

Herein lies just a glimpse of the many faces I saw displayed by my own suffering, dear, and loving father. We in the immediate family were all made to both suffer for his angry, often psychotic, and unpredictable outbursts and yet to feel comfort in his expressively generous and kind heart. He was most definitely a feared and beloved father as well as a man full of renaissance knowledge. All sciences, medicine and psychology, four languages, poetry, religion, global cultures, history, and anthropology were among his interests and ongoing studies.

How could my fascination for his intellectual brilliance and appreciation for his providential and giving heart find harmony with my fear of him? In his worst years, he would leave butcher knives as bookmarks when I was a child less than 5 years old. Yet, his genuine and loving encouragement of our own studies and learning was evident in his providence for our education and interest in what fascinated me. He sent me to piano lessons, and always encouraged me to sing for God. But our joy in being with him was buffeted against his unforeseen rage that spewed out in random moments, with no precursor to ever warn us. My sister and I were always left with a disturbed wonder and unresolved despair. I became a master of creating emotional defenses when just a small child. Nothing I did made him truly happy, and I grew up to believe it was my own fault. Thus, my beloved father's sufferings were not only stuffed deep within my flesh and mind, but they also mutated into new and even uglier faces, by way of my own learned ego/emotional addictions.

***

Negative Emotions Seen Through the Lens of the Holy Spirit

Let us identify God's Reality of the more important spiritual truths regarding this part of my family's story. I have clearly outlined that the source of my father's negative emotional mind was the result of his absorption of the sufferings resulting from warfare, poverty, and his own family's inability to seek and stay in communion with God through it all. He was not to blame for such things that were out of his control, but he was responsible for his own decisions regarding the degree to which he Renewed his own mind in Faith in Jesus Christ.

Negative emotions are frequencies brought forth in thought by the devil while he had his brief sojourn of dominion in this world. Lucifer was a wily, creative, beautiful and brilliant angel who was the original being to create the frequencies of covetous jealousy toward and of God. He wanted to be God in full, not just to possess His Graces, which were the gifts given to him individually, by God. He intentionally allowed these disconnected energies within his own mind, and then brought forth the frequency wavelength of "lack" to the mind of mankind because he knew that he could never be God. He wanted a "pay back" of revenge against God and sought to make

God's newest creation, humanity, bear the brunt of his wrath, and to be subject to his own evil dominion as well.

This "lack" is better described as an actual energetic and cosmic cut in the supernatural connection between a person and God Almighty. Lucifer knew that in order to seize control of the new civilizations being brought forth on Earth, he would have to make the humans believe that God was not around for them. He wanted them to forget that they even ever had a connection to Him. To begin with, he would have to destroy their belief in both creation and eternal existence. From this cosmic cut called, "lack," the myriad of other negative emotional frequencies were brought forth and became entrenched in the way humanity thinks and perceives of itself in the ongoing plague of disconnection. Hatred, jealousy, greed, rage, lust, covetousness, sexual perversion, anxiety, depression, life-long sorrow—any and all negative emotional frequencies have their ultimate source in that fallen angel.

However, the greater Truth IS, and forever shall be this: Satan is a bound and defeated devil—a REALITY that popular Christianity in the churches does not collectively embody (and thus chooses to reject) because there is no collective living of this part of God's Truth. Were this not so, there should not be a single person on the face of this Earth, who calls himself or herself a Christian, who is suffering in any way. This was part of the Purpose and the intended result of Christ's most holy Sacrifice and Atonement, according to the Mind of Christ.

Our Lord Jesus Christ whipped and BOUND the devil 1,982 years ago at the age of 33. Upon Crucifixion, the Divinely supernatural Blood and Water of the body of

Jesus SATURATED not just this world, but the WHOLE of the dimension in which Earth resides. His Blood is the Nourishment of all ages, before and beyond all time, and He chose to have it spilled, along with the Holy Water from His Flesh, so that the Atonement would be made physically manifest and available for all mankind, then and now. It was not just Sacrificial, but His Precious Blood is the very embodiment of Heavenly Wisdom, supernatural Knowledge, cosmic Mysteries, immediate Healing and the very blueprint of all Life. When the drips of His sweat came as Blood in the Garden of Gethsemane, when His Blood oozed out of His blistering back from the whippings, when His Precious Crown was punctured by the crown of thorns, His Blood was touching ALL LIFE BEYOND ALL TIME, in His Indomitable Love.

Now, the Blood that dripped from His Holy Body when His veins and arteries were ripped open by thick iron nails had a slightly different Healing effect and purpose for mankind's future. Jesus was getting closer to the moment when he would descend into hell to encounter the devil, and the knock on that evil door came with each pounding of the hammer that drove the nails into the beloved wrists and feet of the Holiest of Holies.

Three nails driven by mankind into God the ONE, God the SON, and God the Holy Spirit. The Tree used for His Cross was shaped in the four directions, and even though all saw upon it the tortured body of a man, Jesus the Christ used His Cross to radiate His supernaturally Divine Light unto all dimensions, throughout all universes. He was not just saving humanity. He was cleansing the whole of outer space, because evil had touched all of it except Heaven.

Then, the deluge of Water, which poured forth from His side after the sword sliced Him, supernaturally made manifest His Promise of eternal Life for those who would choose thus, for it drenched the whole of the Earth in His unique Energetic Perfection and Purpose.

Jesus did not just die for your sins and those of all mankind. He died to Heal you and to bring you back into His Infinite Heart, Body, and Mind.

Let us not forget that it was Jesus alone Who went full force, straight into hell to defeat the one originally responsible for all of mankind's woes. Jesus' very light made the devil cower in submission. Our Lord could have annihilated him on the spot. Why didn't He?

Jesus did not destroy the devil because His LOVE for humankind gave birth to the FAITH that His Children would choose to reject evil and embrace Him. He paved the way in His Grace and with His gift of Free Will for people to discover themselves as belonging to the Christ alone, not the ways of the devil. He wanted people to taste of themselves as spirit beings in the pure possession of God Almighty, and for them to remember that the Earth was no one's true home.

So the Christ SEVERED the bonds that were energetically binding ALL of mankind to hell, doing away completely and eternally with the dominion of satan's stranglehold on Earth. Jesus destroyed the cosmic and spiritual chains of death, disease, and all other wages of sin, from the body, soul and spirit of mankind. FOREVER.

It is now up to each and every individual human being to make the choice to Receive His most Precious Body of Truth into his or her own being. This is what would ensure that Infinity could be experienced, even while in human form, even while living in this world.

I suggest you take a moment now, to re-read the passage above so as to let the COMMAND of His Grace and Indomitable Might overpower the whole of your being. His Awesome Love is for you.

This is a world of evil, and it thrives on the comforts of disconnection, which is all things born of ego addictions: materiality, superficiality, self-centeredness, oppression, etc. All beings fall short of the Glory of God.

***

FROM A ROCK TO A PEARL IN GOD'S OCEAN OF HEALING

My own precious father, whose soul was so abused yet who had a true heart of Gold, could not shake himself free in Faith of God's WORD. He did not know the loving communion of belonging to Jesus Christ, Who is the ONLY Source of Goodness, Truth, and Life. His mind, at first, did not soften enough to let his heart see beyond the pollutions of his own mental creation, so as to release the hurts of what he was born into and of those he witnessed.

My father miraculously put himself through medical school, came to America, married my mother, had my sister and me, and chose to remain stuck in a mind/body filthy with the stuffed frequencies of a defeated devil as he built his worldly life as an American, a father and a doctor. And yet, his loving heart shone through for me in constant providence and in sacred fatherly activity. Despite the hellish rays from him, so commonly displayed throughout my childhood, I loved him fearfully, and endearingly.

I was raised by this dedicated and loving man whose addictions to the frequencies of emotional lies eventually got the best of his physical heart, bringing forth his body's death at the early age of 60.

I have given you this brief summary of my father to highlight why he was not able, as a parent, to then properly guide his own daughter who had destroyed herself prompted by the same sorrows and despair that he carried, albeit with a slightly different look. His lack of direction to care for me seems understandable given his shock and horror, combined with the fact that in 1997, the year of my suicide, he was just two years away from his own physical death in 1999.

Had he been truly able to listen to the Holy Spirit's guidance, he would have sought to over-run my mother's decision to place me in an adult outpatient day care program at a city psychiatric hospital in the months following my suicide. He would have sought Christian psychiatrists, psychologists, counselors, trusted priests—someone whose soul was conversant with the Holy WORD that Heals all—to be the ones to assist me in that very dark hour of need.

But he didn't, and the other, worldly decision was made manifest.

For three months as a pained 20-year-old soul I was brought to an adult psychiatric day care unit, to be surrounded by severely addicted drug users on parole, delusional schizophrenics, and depressive, nearly comatose individuals. The old German psychiatrist of whom my mother thought so highly appeared for only 30 minutes out of that seven hour-long day care, speaking in his thick German accent of how the synapses and receptors of the brain are chemically out of balance when "we are depressed or thinking thoughts that are not normal."

And "You are on these medications because your chemical imbalance is being corrected."

And "You must take your medications most likely for the rest of your life as the body is made like a machine that needs certain adjustments."

These lies they fed me only fortified the shackles upon my soul. When a soul is starved for Truth and Remembrance, it will typically absorb poison further. A pained soul will never Return to its knowing as a spirit being when it is bombarded by others who serve the evils of the world in making a career of mankind's ego-centric knowledge and mica-thin mind and have no intention to nurture the soul in Christ's Indomitable Love.

I caution you: never seek counsel from one who has no personal conviction and profession of the Almighty Love and Truth of God.

My spirit still maintained a burning spark within my being, and I fought all of those lies, but with great difficulty. My true Self did not accept nor believe one word that came out of any of those psychologists or psychiatrists, for they oozed the false-face righteousness of their claim to the supremacy of medical science above and beyond anything of Truth or heart. They themselves knew nothing of their own spirits, let alone their souls, but relied on their own degrees and studies of the chemical and mechanical patterns of the brain as well as the American Psychiatric Association's latest edition of diagnostic manuals to "treat" their patients.

My spirit was working under an oppressive bombardment from without and within during this time. My mind, conscious and subconscious, was already weary from years of defensive protection against the inundation of distrust, neglect, and from a lack of embodied Unconditional Love. The bonds within and around my whole being were thick with lies that had saturated my mind and heart.

Most people cannot see it, but there truly is a darkened and thick body of energy surrounding one who is plagued in the mind, heart and body. As a child, it is received from the adults all around, but as one grows into adulthood, it mutates, taking on new layers and faces, and becomes one's personal "property", part of the personal identity and character. (I will refer to this, later in the book, as an "ego-ism.") This cosmic sludge becomes a magnet for more evildoers and other unclean hearts, feeding the world with their dark frequencies.

For one who is dis-eased in heart and mind, it takes a core-strength, resolution, and at least a tiny spirit flame of the Love of God to unite with the Miracle of God's Redemption and Salvation.

I remember the day when the young male social worker guiding the group after lunch looked at a file with my name on it, then at me and said, "You do not belong here. You are 20 years old, and you need to get yourself together, overcome what binds you and go live." This apparent cliché was actually a powerful expression. In the next moment, I revisited everything I had seen upon leaving my body at death. I saw the ocean of crystal Pink, White, and Gold Light, I felt the washing of God's Love for me, and I saw both the vision of my own Children as well as the endless stream of beings that I was destined to assist. At that moment, I got an extra dose of Awareness of my original purpose for being on this planet, for work that I had long before committed to do. There was an electrical charge that whooshed through me such as I had never before experienced.

I stood up and walked out of that building, a flame ignited.

The Holy Spirit always finds the most perfect way to radiate what needs to be sent forth, using any particular person or circumstance to make His Will be appropriately Received, according to God's singular Will. It is ready to happen, but only at the very moment when God sees the perfection in a situation or circumstance among individuals. Like a trickling stream or lightning bolt from the sky, God always has God's Way.

Be confident and know this: if you give your mind/body/soul to Christ in every moment, He Will be there in some fashion to Guide, no matter what your physical circumstances may seem. He will only shower upon and through you that which He is clearly aware you can handle, taking it by degree, but always one step further in Faith.

Yes, I jumped up and threw that false-face world of talking mannequins into the fire, but I still did not speak the Name of Jesus the Christ in repentance. I did quietly pray to the "Great Spirit," saying that I was ready to embark upon a path of Renewal, desiring to start my life all over. Even though I had been trained as a Catholic child to confess my sins and to seek the Father's Intercession for my life, I had been stripped of my knowing of BELONGING to God Almighty in permeation, and I had nearly forgotten about my personal relationship with Jesus.

But in spite of all that, God's tender Mercy was still showering upon me. *Praise God!*

I weakly asked God to have all negative memories of my past erased from my conscious mind, and that I be given the Healing and power to return to college, which I had left after my freshman year 2 years before. I knew that I had to be free of what was lodged in my mind in order to be able to proceed for the future, and that the easiest way to distance myself from the intensity of it was to Pray that it all just be wiped away from my thinking mind. Well, God would acknowledge and make that Prayer manifest, but only to a minimal degree, for one must become the Muscle of the Holy Spirit, in the willingness to do the work that is required of a Prayer requested of God. And freeing the psychosis of the subconscious mind is no easy task without a full communion in Christ!

I acknowledged the visions I had been given upon death, and stated that my heart was ready to begin to Re-learn how to be a Mother. I so deeply wanted those Children of mine, but I was honest about not knowing at all how to nurture myself.

I did have a biological mother, but she was the one who had put me in the psychiatric ward and had not willfully worked me back into the Hands of God. Yes, she had taken care of me physically to the best of her ability. Yes, she loved me in her own way, but she never chose to grow in Christ. In fact, she had grown up believing in the Lord under the guidance of her own Christ-focused parents, but as a young adult she became enamored with seeing life through the lens of politics and social structures. She focused on inequalities between men and women, race issues, class issues, but never did she give her attention to the truth that mankind had fractured itself by collectively disowning Jesus, creating its own iniquities. She even came to reject Christ as the Savior, the only Son of God, calling him just a "really good teacher," which causes God to grieve.

But my dear and kind mother was also the one who horrifically found my body on that cold garage floor of Good Friday 1997. As the mother I am now, I cannot imagine the hell of such a discovery. I have great love and compassion for her because of what I know of her life, soul, and yes, even her spirit. Part of my Breathing Prayer is to see her Redemption and Salvation and Healing. For it is God's Will that all who would choose thus, be Healed.

Oh how precious, enduring, and endearing is our God! By His Mercy I was rescued and yanked back into a body whose subconscious and conscious mind was still riddled with stuffed negative emotional frequencies, whose physical and soulful Healing needs were still so great! The task and journey before me in Reconnection to my spirit (as well as a full Return to Christ) was to be a tumultuous and perilous ride.

***

THE LOOK OF THE HEALING: GOD'S ESSENCE THROUGH NATURE

How does one who is so lost nurture oneself? How could I possibly be given the gift of Motherhood when I possessed no True Love of my own being, and no real understanding of the Love of God Almighty? How could I return to the mundane rhythms of a personal life, seeking some sort of fit in a disconnected world that would only endeavor to keep me ever more disconnected?

So much sweetness had been revealed to me by the supernatural Divine! Would that Miracle of His Mercy and Healing be enough for my soul to overcome the lies still entrenched within the mind? Where was the balance to be found between having been gifted something so spiritually powerful, and a conscious mind that was just beginning to properly function again? Who would be there in the flesh to directly guide me upon a straight and narrow path that would lead to self-realization in ELOI, the One God?

All of the answers to these questions would unfold, manifesting in the next few years after the suicide and Return. But it was the physical Healing that was most immediate, profound, and impossibly brought forth by the ONLY ONE WHO IS capable of such power. To God alone I give all the Praise and all the Glory!

My body's healing was quick, but the initial symptoms were intense. For three days after the Return from suicide, my heart experienced extreme atrial fibrillation. My heart rate would accelerate to 190 beats per minute (bpm) for minutes at a time, and then slow to 35 bpm for minutes at a time. There was no consistency. I was in a coma for the first 2 days after I came back into body, and this perilous heart condition was watched round the clock, as was my brainwave activity. There was no telling at that point, what kind of brain damage I might have incurred, as I was not conscious. But on that third day, I came out of the coma, my heart rate balanced out to a rate of 78 bpm, and I was definitely aware of who and where I was.

Right now I acknowledge in sacred devotional love, the Glory of our God in this particular aspect of the Healing. You, ELOI, Who took command of my every atom, my every cell, working through the materiality of the third dimension by way of Your boundless Power. You Healed my flesh in such an impossibly quick space of time. I bear Witness in personal testimony unto the holy Water of your WORD and Will; this supernaturally Divine energy washed through that body with such cleansing and nourishing Perfection. No man, no doctor, and no positive affirmation is capable of such Majesty. ONLY YOU, GOD, ONLY YOU.

Five days after the Return, I was discharged from the hospital fully able to walk, breathe, and eat, with a heart rate that had stabilized to a constant 72 bpm, but the True Healing was far from complete.

There was no sense of awe in my heart and mind for what I had been given. I felt no constant expression of

Gratitude at all for having a body Rebirthed and Restored. Occasionally, I wondered, "Why me? Why was I given this?"

And in my conscious mind's dis-eased state, what with the stuffed emotions and unresolved issues still leaking from my subconscious mind into my daily thinking mind, the sacred awareness of my spirit in relation to what I had seen on the Other Side would flicker as a fading light bulb in the battle of my thoughts. Overwhelming waves of depression consumed me in those months when I was forced to attend the psychiatric outpatient day care. A numbed constancy of disinterest in just about everything brought a dull stupor to my demeanor. Since my thoughts often were incongruous, and I had nobody to talk to except my mother, stepfather, and sister, I kept everything stuffed deeply inside. I never picked up my once-loved guitar, never sang, never drew to bring forth art the way I had in the past. There were weeks on end in those first months following the suicide where I would just stare at one space of a wall, responding to no one, even if they spoke to me.

Then the Holy Spirit got a hold of me through the Sunshine's cosmic force of God's accessible Body, as presented via Nature on this Earth. Nature's grasp pulled me outside, and when I was finally given some personal freedom away from my mother and stepfather's constant physical monitoring, I took walks around the suburban neighborhood where one of the houses of my Childhood (which was the same as the house of my death) still stands to this day. I escaped to nearby wilderness reserve parks, where bubbling brooks spoke mysteries that I could not interpret, but whose lilting serenades soothed the whole of me in those tender summer days.

I sought the rays of the Sunshine daily. And because I wanted to encounter no human being, I did my best to go as deep into the woods as I could possibly go. I watched each trunk of every Tree as I walked by, placing my attention on the reality of their roots extending so much further than the eye could behold. I found it in me to say, "Thank you," to these beings whose constant gracious gift of oxygen filled the whole of me and of all on this planet.

A particular brook where I had stolen away as a Child to read was a common destination in those initial months of Healing. There was a huge White Oak I had named "Scylla", after Scylla and Charybdis of Homer's Odyssey. The roots of this majestic Tree extended out from the banks of the brook, protruding so that the Tree was partially suspended in the air. As a child, I would sit on the flattened spot right at the curve where the trunk accelerated vertically into the Blue sky and swim my legs in the air over the Water. I saw those gigantic roots as I coincidingly envisioned Scylla, the many-legged beast of the great ocean that Odysseus fought single-handedly. Together, Odysseus and I rode oceans unseen to the world. But I also needed to change Homer's story a bit for my own soul medicine.

In Homer's story, she and her watery twin, Charybdis, were the bad guys. Part of my Childhood psychology was to take something bad and make it good because it was my way of trying to make sense of what I was going through with my raging daddy and confused mother. I was giving up trying to make them happy and trying to change them, so I turned to what I knew I could create: the workings of my spirit visioning.

Children are brilliant artists within the spirit world, and every opportunity should be given to foster and nurture this aspect of their own unique spirits, for maintaining creative and artistic expression usually assists a Child to remain open to the Holy Spirit, no matter what happens along the way.

Imagination was not fantasy to me. I knew that what I could see internally was more real than what I experienced in the world. This was my spirit's understanding, and as a young Child I had a definite connection to who I really am. It was easier to find solace in my spirit visioning than it was to go back to the house where I lived with adults who had no idea who they really were. Still, I maintained my itching awareness that I was not from this world by way of Nature. That was to change quickly in the next years when, somehow, the self-induced mental demons got the better of me for a space of time. In those moments in Nature, the Holy Spirit caused me to return to visions from my Childhood.

I want to stress that the positive visual memories of the past that come through are a necessary part of everyone's Healing; for a dis-eased mind must recall some time—any time—where the frequencies of Goodness were experienced in a given life so as to provide an elixir for the illusions of dis-ease in the present moment.

As my thinking mind softened under the influence of the Sunlight and water mixing together in the serenade of the bubbling brook, my breath carried me to memories of a powerful spiritual helper in the form of a beloved animal who had graced my Childhood. I belonged to many pets over the years, but I share with you here only about Shawn. He is a powerful warrior of Christ's Healing, and I want you to benefit from meeting him now, by way of this happy story from my Childhood.

When I was 6 years old, my father decided to get a German Shepherd. We lived on a significant acreage of land at that time, and he wanted a protector dog, not a companion for the family. I was shocked when daddy decided that Shawn was too big and hairy to live in the house with us, and that he would spend his days leashed up to the barn near the house.

"NOOOOO! You cannot do that to Shawn! If he is to live here with us, he is to LIVE here, daddy!"

My vehement expressions on the verge of tantrums never made any change. Daddy just ignored my objections and told me just to feed Shawn every day instead. I was outraged and horrified, considering my daddy to be the most evil man on the planet because of his decision to neglect Shawn, so I made a plan.

One would think that Shawn would have become a most angry and aggressive dog, being tied up the way he was, day in and day out. There was some shelter from the rain and snow, as he could slip into the barn for protection, but there was no additional warmth. Despite the abuse of neglect, Shawn was the most gracious of gentlemen to me. And I adored him.

Everyday I would come out with his giant silver bowl of Purina chow, which I secretly topped with melted coconut oil. I tried to think of additional ways I could make his food more exciting, so I would scrape fish leftovers from the cooking skillets, melt coconut oil, or rip up uneaten chicken bits and mix that into the kibbles. Shawn loved it, and I know he loved it more because I would approach him in great fanfare, putting on a singing show so as to present his food to him as the "lord of the land". He never jumped, never got overly excited. For if he had, his 110-pound body would have caused serious damage to my six year old self!

Just feeding Shawn did not provide nurturing enough for my little soul's needs. For that 6-year-old who tried to run away from the house every time her daddy had one of his mysterious raging fits, when glasses would fly through the air and smash against walls—and when no one would say a word in response to his demonic outbursts out of great fear—there was just one solution: run with Shawn and imagine, imagine, IMAGINE.

Little did I know in those moments of time, what that beloved spirit being in German shepherd form was really providing for me. Shawn KNEW exactly what was going on. When he saw me running out of the house, sometimes in tears, other times breathless with fear, he stood guard, waiting for me. I would quickly untether his leash, and we would RUN. Or rather, Shawn would run me.

It must have been quite a sight to see that little six year old trying to maintain pace with that gigantimo of a dog. Often he was practically dragging me, but I did not care one bit. Instantly, his passionate zeal for freedom consumed me and washed me clean in JOY, and my hand stayed latched on to that leash by the Grace of God.

We lived on a few acres of land, so sometimes I would look behind my shoulder and in all directions to make sure no one was watching me and simply unhooked Shawn from his leash. Here's where the magic unfolded.

Shawn had this internal spiritual GPS about our destination every single time. He knew he was assigned to me, to help me see God's Love, and he would run like the wind, stop to look back to see how close I was to him, and then take off again. I was ecstatic with glee to be free and wild with him, and that first time he was loose, I had no idea where we were going.

The land was rugged with woods at the outer edges of those acres, and Shawn knew of another bubbling brook surrounded by Oaks and lined with perfect sitting Rocks for him and myself. It was a mini Never-Never land, with lush Green mosses lining the rocks, and strange delicate Pink flowers dotting the sides of the brook. The Water looked so clear and perfect, as it was straight from the Ozark Mountains the land was a part of. Shawn ripped space to get there, but then came to a dignified trot as soon as we were 25 feet away. I know now that he was stoically greeting the spirit beings of the Trees, the Water, and the Rocks, announcing our arrival. He would then jump into the brook, and I followed suit immediately. He would splash me with both paws, putting on his own grand show as he stood on his haunches to accomplish that gymnastic feat. We would play like this for hours, and then come to rest on the rocks in sheer exhaustion. Amazingly, none of my family ever came looking for me in those summer days. That spot was exclusively reserved and protected, for Shawn and me. In those heavenly moments, I completely forgot about the horrors at home, and had no care in the world weighting my little being. Oh, what a grand and blissful getaway it was, every single time. My beloved Shawn holds his earned place in

Heaven, and I look forward to our reunion jaunts in the starry bubbling brooks of God's Abode.

If you are not creating joyful memories in your present life, then you must allow Christ to Heal your heart by recalling times of bliss, however infrequent or minimal they were. This is the one area of the past where it is wise and good to intentionally recall, if you do not find yourself naturally drifting to those times.

I highly recommend that if you have never belonged to a domesticated animal, you do so in your present life. I do not care what kind of mental strife you are going through, a pet is from God's Heart in His Purity, and if your intention is to connect with one, God will send you a spiritual helper who may very well remain with you for eternity. It is now my knowing that Shawn's spirit became a part of my soul, and would be part of the REAL spiritual medicine team to help me through the rest of my arduous Healing journey, even after he left his own body. I love you and thank you, my dear Buddy and Peace warrior, Shawn!

As an older Child, around 10 years, I would also escape into Nature through swimming. There are photos of myself from those summers, all tanned and happy in the Golden Sun, never ever wanting to go inside. Many days, I swam from morning till twilight, taking breaks to use the bathroom and eat. I imagined mermaids and dolphins, great Blue whales and jellyfish, swimming alongside me in our backyard pool. I did not have any close Childhood friends, so my imagination was my traveling universe, and it was most definitely another ray of Christ's medicine to see me through those tumultuous years.

Being born in a blizzard, I have come to think of that as the reason I have a fixation and passion for Snow. Starting from around age two, I adopted a practice of running in the Winter freezes as the grounds were layered in feet of the beloved crystals, dressed only in a t-shirt and shorts, and with bare feet. It was sheer delight, much to the horror of my parents.

Finally, gardening was another saving grace for my tender mind, and herein I can also clearly identify that Nature was a medicine bridge between my father and me —a bridge born of Christ's design, to be sure. For Daddy had such knowledge and wisdom regarding the growing of flowers and vegetables, and he shared it all with me. Some of my earliest happy memories are of trailing after him through the extensive gardens he had built from nothing, bugging him with questions, and helping him plant seeds. I adored harvesting the giant *umpalaya*, or bitter squash, cucumbers, tomatoes, spinach, and more that he loved to plant every year.

For years now I have continued in his legacy, building upon and maintaining family gardens of our own, teaching my children what I know and have learned along the way.

Despite the trauma and the heartache of parts of my Childhood, the sacred spirit beings embodied in the gardens and all the Animals I have ever belonged to have always been part of God's Healing strength made manifest for me. I want you to reflect upon the sacred relationships you have or have had with any beloved Animal who has blessed your life, and stand in awe of such a heavenly Gift of Healing. Let us Give Thanks for such wondrous blessings!

Again, this same nourishment radiates unto you in every word I write. *Praise God!*

***

BACK TO WEEKS OF POST RESURRECTION AND MORE NATURE MEDICINE

There is only ONE Resurrection that truly matters, and it is most certainly not mine. I have always hesitated to use the word "resurrection" to describe what God gave me by bringing me back from the hell of suicide death, because in the past, I have never ever wanted to compare anything of my life experiences to those of Jesus the Christ. My awareness that addiction to things of ego can easily take on new faces has always propelled me to use different words to describe what I went though, for spiritual ego is one of the most evil of all false faces. Nothing of Goodness is born of the individual, no matter how dedicated one is to Christ. It ALL belongs to God Almighty. And one who uses Words from the Holy Bible had better have a walk that reflects such sacred Fruit.

But here's the thing: Jesus DOES want us to compare our life experiences with His. He yearns for more individuals to model everything about their lives after His Way, His Word, and His Teachings. The fact that billions of Earth residents choose to live and think opposite to the way of Jesus, is the very reason why humanity is presently set upon the path of annihilating itself in Eternity. In addition to imitating Him, welcoming Him to live THROUGH the whole of one's being, one must ALWAYS give God alone, all the credit, all the Praise, and

ALL the Glory. In this way, the Holy Spirit can take over the personal life even more, and thus make God's Will manifest through one more individual on Earth.

Thus, I have changed what I realized was, in itself, an ego-centric attitude: that of *not* wanting to use the word "resurrection" to describe what God did for me and through me. I certainly was not going to give all the Glory to the team at the hospital, although I am eternally grateful to each of them. And of course, I myself had absolutely no power in any of it. Coming back from the dead, by way of Jesus Christ, IS indeed a resurrection. All Praise and Glory unto He Who Lives!

The very nature of living in communion with the Christ is also gifted by God through Nature's medicine on Earth, and there is not a single being on this planet who does not benefit from the sacred manifestations of God's Love by way of it.

Although my conscious mind was still not "normal" in functioning continuous thoughts in April and May of 1997—as experienced by myself and certainly by others when attempting conversation—my soul was finding solace in all these places of sacred Nature. It was a place I understood and which I knew understood me.

I found the magic spots in between the Trees where the Sun's rays seeped onto the rocks and water. There I would just sit and Receive the warm nourishment of God's whisperings made manifest in solar light. In those spots of God's direct permeation, I would speak to ELOI in Quietude in my own non-cognitive way of yearning and communicating.

Great Spirit, I know you are here, and yet I still LONG for You. I have no clue how to get to You as fully as I want to. For I want to just jump out of this torture and be free right now! But the despair is so real. How do I get out of this? What do I do? What will make this better now?

Nothing but the bubbling and faithful stream answered me. Often feeling cheated and expecting that there should be some kind of Voice I could detect, sometimes ego would bring forth anger at God for "depriving" me of an understandable and interpretable response, to which I felt entitled because of that one gracious act of Mercy given upon death.

"Yeah, go ahead, then. Stay silent. I am totally alone in this. I screwed up, killed myself, and now my punishment is to go it alone, with no supernatural light, no visions like I had. I am just going to have to forge my way through this nonsense then, eh? Thanks. Thanks a lot."

The nasty sarcasm and ingratitude of ego coupled with fear prevented me, in those moments, from truly Receiving the Healing guidance that was being given in answer to my entreaties. But I kept coming back to those spots in Nature, kept taking those walks, kept doing my best to get away from the past as much as possible. But until the past is thrown fully into the Living Fire of the Holy Spirit, the unrepentant mind and heart will continue to be dis-eased by its trappings.

And yet, the Hand of God was still working as the dominant Fire in my life, for I was destined to become a mother of three, and a Mother for all.

***

The Rocky Healing Continues

In August of 1998, just a year after my death and Return, I re-enrolled in college as a sophomore at the University of Missouri in Columbia. With a commitment to beginning anew, and really believing that all of my past had just been completely zapped out of existence, I went forth. God gave me enough of a healed brain and conscious mind to be focused and ready for the major change I was muscling into reality. And that is an understatement of the look of how Creator healed my body in those amazing weeks.

The time in which my nervous system was healed was miraculous. You do the math: In March of 1997, I had turned myself into a mental vegetable, oxygen deprivation and brain damage had rendered me unable to make complete sentences or think a full thought. By August of 1998, I was fully able and ready to return to a full honors university study program.

There had been no medical treatment for my brain or heart at that. If you want to call the psychiatric drugs they tried to administer to me, "medicine", then go right ahead. (Even though I was forced to have my blood taken once a week to monitor the toxicity levels of one of the "medicines" they thought I was taking, I routinely flushed most of them down the toilet. One hour before the test, I would pop one of the pills just to make sure they could see what they wanted to.) But there was no allopathic treatment for my inability to talk, nor any monitoring of my heart, post discharge from the hospital. It was all God's Radiance—then, now, and Forever.

I resumed where I had left off in my studies of History, Anthropology, and Women Studies, this time choosing to take on 18 hours of honors courses as opposed to the 12 hours I had started with, in my freshman year. I moved into a dormitory, made some new friends, and reconnected with some old ones I had left a year prior. No one had known where I had gone or what had happened. I discussed it with nobody, except to say that I had needed to get away and had "gone on a little trip". In some ways, I really believed that this was so, as I had told God that I was dutifully burning the past away from me. Relying on positive affirmations, fed like Kool-Aid to myself morning, noon, and night as I looked into a mirror and spoke them, I was psyching myself into believing that I had the power to overcome everything that had been, and that nothing would ever keep me down ever again.

Poor, silly little thing I was in that shallow and ridiculous ego-born will!

The ego is a cunning thing, and because I also had a small degree of attunement to my spirit, there was a strange combination of TRUE will to thrive and grow mixed with the plaguing horrors of an un-cleansed heart and filthy subconscious mind. That self-induced addiction was about to hit me hard for the second and last time.

I was going to school in a college town 120 miles away from my dear father, Pacelli Escondo Brion, who was on his dying path in St. Louis, Missouri. In that fall of 1998, it would be exactly one more year when he would forever leave his body. In my "newly created life" I chose to have very little communication with him, as there were too many painful things I did not want to admit regarding my Childhood and his rage. I knew he was dying, but I did not know how to face that fact in addition to all of the discord still lurking inside the deepest parts of my mind.

But oh, how I loved him. I loved how he taught me about the sanctity of Nature. I loved him for providing for my sister and me. I loved his soulful singing and piano playing. I loved his ridiculous Andre Bocelli imitation. I loved his devotion to Life. I loved his devotion to helping others to self-realization by way of the profession he had chosen as an unconventional medical doctor and psychiatrist. I loved him because of the proof of his love for other people in the hundreds who showed up for his wake and funeral, as well as the many personal testimonies I heard from people who shared intimate details of how Daddy assisted their soul and spirit, not just their minds. I loved him for all of that and so much more. My soul knew his soul, but greater than that, my spirit knew his spirit, and he was the only one in my life who really did his best to show me that I really am not of this world ... in God's Truth and Everlasting Body.

It was disturbing to me to think about his heart destroying itself in that evil congestive heart failure. I Prayed for his complete Healing. But at that time in my development, I blamed it all on him for holding on to such sorrow and expressing it as rage unto his Children. I was so confused in how to feel about him, so I chose not to think of him at all, keeping my focus and attention completely on my studies and securing the straight As I was used to. Making the dean's honor roll was a lot simpler than facing the self-induced demons who were allowed to make camp in my tender psyche. When I observed myself succeeding in making such good grades, as well as acting in four major theatrical productions on campus in one year, those nasty frequencies inside me were allowed to fester deep within, until ...

Slowly, I began to wither, as the awareness of my father's impending death grew. I had no control over his destiny, and felt the horror of losing my strange and beloved daddy. I began to restrict my eating and to engage in excessive exercise as the internal pressure of all those pent-up emotions began to manifest outwardly as anorexia. From winter of 1998 onward I began to lose weight rapidly. As my father was waning from this world, my addictions of ego—most certainly a part of the work of the minions of evil—wanted me to do exactly the same.

It was on the bright, warm, sunny afternoon of August 24, 1999 as I was bicycling back to the rented house I shared with my boyfriend (who had proposed marriage to me) that I felt a wrenching in my gut so hard that I crashed, falling off my bike. I knew my father had died.

I got back on my bike, and pedaled weakly the rest of the way to our house where my boyfriend told me that my sister had just called.

"I know. My dad is dead."

I bypassed his embrace and headed straight for the bedroom and shut the door. There were no tears, just the rumble of an empty stomach and a nearly non-existent heart.

We traveled to St. Louis for the wake and funeral services. It was during the visitation hours with the open casket that the second supernatural occurrence of my life took place.

In traditional Filipino custom, each person approached the open casket to kneel in Prayer, and any Children of the deceased always went after the widow. My own biological mother and he had divorced when I was 8 months old. So it was my stepmother who came forward. She was a native Filipina woman and had been faithful and enduring to my father since their marriage when I was six years old.

She kneeled first beside the coffin in quiet Prayer. Shedding sweet tears as she rose to her feet, she kissed my father's cheek one last time, and turned away. Next, my older sister approached the casket. I sat off to the side, both dreading and anticipating my turn, never expecting what happened next.

All eyes were upon me, as my sister had already knelt, Prayed, stood, and returned to her seat next to me. Some minutes had passed before I realized it was my turn to "say goodbye." The white *Sampaguita,* Jasmine, and Bird of Paradise flowers, his favorites, surrounding him were so beautiful, so perfect. The whole of my being began to ache with despair seeing my tai, my daddy, as just that dead body lying there, surrounded by such exquisite life.

I stood up, shaking, and made my way over to the casket to kneel before him. I used the edge of the casket for support to get on my knees, looking down as my legs descended onto the cushion. Then I looked up at his unnatural painted face, the formaldehyde–pumped body stiff in a suit that he had never worn, lying in a casket that would take hundreds of years to decompose. I was staring at a mannequin made to look like my Daddy.

And then he moved—My father's dead body moved in that casket.

I saw very clearly his whole head turn, with eyes closed, first to the left, then to the right, and then back to center. My body began to shake, as if there was a current of electricity streaming through me as my eyes practically popped out of my skull. I was filled with ecstatic joy, confusion, and expectation that he was about to jump out of the casket and join everyone in the room where the huge spread of food was. I turned around gingerly, desperately wanting to observe any other person in the room who may have seen what I saw, but not wanting to call attention to myself at the same time. I was both shocked and also felt perfectly normal about this very real supernatural occurrence. I knew I was still messed up inside, but I had no doubt at all that what I had just seen had really happened. My proof was the currents of electricity that were surging up and down my body. That was not at all "normal." As I kept my gaze upon my father's flesh, the currents remained strong. When I looked away from him, they faded in tangibility. As sick as I was in my psyche, my soul and spirit were still in the possession of our Supernaturally Divine God, and He wanted me to KNOW that this was real. God was burning through me the Reality that there is no death in the Way of Christ Jesus.

My dad had been a known and respected Christian seer of sorts, one in the Filipino community to whom many others came for counsel and who was known to have gifts of tuning into things unseen and tasted by most people only through Faith.

But nobody seemed to be doing anything other than crying or sitting still, looking in the direction of the casket with that general quiet and solemn reverence common to a wake. I turned my focus back to my father's face, as I quietly talked to him.

"So you are not really dead, then, huh daddy?"

The body was perfectly still again, just as it had been—dead.

"What's it gonna be, Tai? How can I say goodbye? I can't. What am I supposed to do? How in the world am I gonna get through this life? How am I supposed to be healed now that you have left me? You were supposed to be here for the day when your first grandchild comes! You are not even going to be here on the day I get married. Why did you do this thing just now? Do you want me to go crazy?! Do you want me to shout out to everyone here that you are not dead? Huh?! ARE YOU DEAD?!!"

A calm stillness swept through my body, and with tears still rolling down my cheeks, I saw just my daddy's face. Yet there was a radiance to his skin that had not been there before. I heard no voice, saw no more supernatural activity, save for the purity of visible peace that emanated from my father's beloved face. His spirit filled me, surrounded me, encapsulated me in the most tender embrace. Just for that moment at least, I was comforted and assured that indeed, his spirit was alive and well.

It would be his spirit that would stay with me, seeing me through to the space I exist within now: the communion of my own soul and spirit unto this mind, heart and body within the liberating possession of God Almighty.

Oh, so much heartache had happened in such a tiny little life, but there I was on the brink of another disaster while Truth was speaking to me still. How long would it take for me to hear and respond with the heart of my spirit?

The scroll of my story will unfold and reveal.

***

Trauma Leading to Triumph

No matter how old you were when such and such trauma happened in your life, no matter how recently the suffering came about by way of your own choices or because of another's ill-will or ignorance, and no matter how scarred you believe yourself to be, Christ is awaiting your Rediscovery that, as a spirit being who is His beloved possession, there is ONLY your ability to Receive all of His most Precious Gifts.

At the age of 37 years in this present physical time, I still spend my every moment focused upon the Healing Rays of Christ.

I want to clarify for you how direly important it is to concentrate on your own Healing needs in Christ, above and beyond all else. In doing so, you are immediately and effectively radiating the Healing Will of God Almighty to all Life, everywhere, no matter what dimension or universe. So you must accept this powerfully interfused declaration of the Holy Spirit:

> YOU BELONG TO THE LIFE, ALL LIFE IS ONE, AND ONLY GOD IS THE WAY, THE TRUTH, AND THE LIFE.

In my sharing of these details of my own story, all Life is immediately, directly, and indirectly saturated with the rays of His Healing Truth. Do you feel His Power in this? *Praise God!*

Oftentimes, trauma to the body has a positive spiritual consequence in that God uses the horror of the incident to jolt a person back into the Truth of who he or she is, as a spirit being, and not exclusively as a human of this world. The course of a person's choices and thoughts, post accident, is what determines the Fruit of Healing and its potential. When trauma happens to a child, it is up to the adult who is responsible for that child, to embody or negate the Will of God for that child's proper spiritual development, according to the adult's degree of attunement to Christ.

The following narrative reveals my daddy's amazing communion in Christ, which was pure and radiant in this true story.

When I was five years old, I experienced a severe head injury, and to this day, I am physically manipulating my upper spine within the Holy Spirit to remove from my being, the last of this lingering physical intensity I have carried. This particular physical Healing is nearly complete, and in the sharing of the encounter—which, on the surface, was brought about by my own sister's insistence and my naive compliance—my flesh becomes fully healed and Christ's Radiance pours forth for all.

***

THE CHRISTMAS SEASON, 1982

My family and I were at our customary Filipino Christmas fiesta. In that particular year it was being held in the gymnasium and the adjacent cafeteria of my own Catholic elementary school. There were more than one hundred people in attendance, as the Filipino community of St. Louis was large and wonderfully connected at that time in my Childhood. Christmas is a huge celebration for Filipinos, who take Worship of the birth of Christ very seriously, and who also know how to throw great parties! There were the usual live traditional music interspersed with someone's horrid karaoke machine—which my dear father loved to command with his singing bravado—the five tables of Filipino and American cuisine spread out buffet-style, laughing people and gleeful children running about. Everyone was in a festive mood, celebrating in the Advent season.

My sister was nine years old at the time, and along with myself, was feeling the jubilant excitement of the moment. Perhaps she and I had been eating too much *leche* flan or *puto* (Filipino desserts), leading to her suggestion of the rash and dangerous activity, and my agreement to participate.

We saw Children doing cartwheels and handstands, as others threw rubber balls in the gymnasium. Dodge ball was in one corner of the gym, while acrobatics of various forms was in another. I jumped into the twirling, cartwheeling flow of Children, mostly girls, as we formed a line, taking organized turns to turn upside down in a most joyful arch, landing safely on our own two feet. My sister watched the mini gymnasts from afar, and then pulled me aside saying, "Elise, I know you can do a regular cartwheel, but have you ever done an aerial one?"

"What's that?" I asked naively and with intense curiosity.

My sister replied, "It's where you back up, get a real good running start, and then you FLIP yourself over in the air, but you don't use your hands on the ground. It's just like a regular cartwheel, 'cuz you will land on your feet, but you don't put your hands on the ground as you flip."

"Wow!" My eyes lit up with the visualization. "But I have never done that before. We have never done that at my gymnastics class." (I had only taken one year of formal gymnastics classes at that time.)

"Oh, you can do it," my sister confidently responded. "Just try it. I will be right here when you flip over to catch you if you need it."

Meanwhile, my father was nowhere in sight, nor was there any direct adult eye upon us as it was a giant party. Had he known of what we had been discussing, he would have immediately nipped that experimental activity in the bud, chastising us both in his native Tagalog tongue, and saved me from the trauma that followed.

I backed up about 25 feet away from my sister, looking around me to be sure no one else was in my running pathway. There were about five other kids standing around as on-lookers, having heard my sister's suggestion and challenge. I took a deep breath and with a smile on my face, took off at five year-old high speed, which is not much.

Two feet before reaching my sister, I crisscrossed my arms grabbing my opposing shoulders to ensure I would not use them for ground support, as I catapulted myself into the motion of a typical cartwheel. Well, I did not jump high enough, nor did I have the proper kinetic energy to make the arch complete, and despite my sister's glowing promises to catch me, she panicked and backed away. I came crashing down, forehead first upon the cement floor of the gymnasium. I blacked out completely, but my spirit saw it all.

I was immediately aware of seeing my little body on the hard, cold floor, and of the pandemonium of a few screaming children and some adults whose attention was directed to the accident. The music stopped and I heard the chaotic shouting of a few adults, "LILLI! LILLI! *Pacelli, pumunta ka rito!*"

"Lilli" was the nickname affectionately given to him by those who knew and loved him.

"Get over here now, Pacelli!" was the concerned command shouted out by my *titas* and *titos*, my aunties and uncles, who had gotten to me first.

Again, I, as my spirit, was observing the whole scene. I saw my father run over to where my body was lying, falling to his knees while shouting in Tagalog for someone to go get some ice. He was a medical doctor and, having been told what had happened in the noisy rush of people all around, wisely cautioned everyone not to move my body out of concern that there had been fractures to my neck or spine. There was an enormous Bluish-Purple hematoma the size of a softball that had formed on my forehead, and I was still unconscious. Yet, I saw my daddy's worried face, perspiring brow, and embodied fatherly love kneeling above my flesh. He very tenderly applied the ice to my head, commanding a few other adults NOT to call 911.

And here's the real Spirit Muscle of medicine that followed:

Being that all present were devout Catholics, my father told everyone to calm down, and kneel around my body in a circle. He immediately began to Pray to God Almighty, first in Tagalog, the official native language of the Philippine islands, and then in English, the Lord's Prayer, in which everyone around me joined in recitation. He had his right hand laid upon the left side of my head at my temple, with his left hand gingerly supporting the ice that was beginning to melt down my face. The others held hands and touched my father's back as they all Prayed together in unison. Word of the accident had spread throughout the rest of the huge Christmas gathering, and the whole of the cafeteria and gym was completely silent except for the comforting chanting of the Prayers uttered aloud.

After about 10 minutes, a friend of my *tai's* asked if he should call the paramedics now, as I was still unconscious. My sweet daddy shook his head "No", and indicated that the Prayer should continue and that there should be no other talk.

Around my body was a group mostly of older women and a few men who were very soulfully close to my family. My daddy continued to lead the Prayer.

"Heavenly Father, we ask your immediate Healing upon Nene. In Jesus' Name, Amen."

"Nene" is the affectionate nickname my daddy had given me at birth, which means "little girl," in Tagalog.

He repeated the same Prayer over and over and over, with the extended family now Prayer-speaking in their own way, some out loud, others quietly. Most of them had their eyes closed.

Another 10 minutes passed as I continued to observe the scene from outside my body, seeing every little detail as described above and more.

In the next five minutes, I came back into my body, into consciousness, opening my eyes. The whole room was spinning, but the first thing that came into view was my *tai's* sweet face immersed in Prayer. He saw me open my eyes, and smiled.

"Thank You, Beloved Father," he spoke quietly.

One *tito* shouted, "Nene is here! Praise God!" which then spread throughout the whole gathering with exclamation of praise and amazement. But I was not out of the woods yet.

I closed my eyes in the delirium of pain as my perception was still a spinning vortex of white walls and jumbled bodies. It was too much for my little five year-old body to bear. I passed out again, but this time within consciousness. I know this because I was very much aware of the pain, and was also aware of the severe concussion. As a little child, however, I had no medical words to describe any of it. All I knew was that everything HURT, a physical memory that is still tangible to this day.

It was an amazing and beautiful experience, as I now reflect on the whole thing.

By the Grace of God Almighty, and through that seemingly horrid accident, my spirit made my little soul aware of what I had come to Earth to do, in this lifetime. I was given future visions regarding my work in this world, and it brought me comfort and peace in the reminder from the Holy Spirit. As I lay there, my spirit and soul became conjoined within that flesh, and I was fully aware of the WHOLE of myself, even though an outside observer saw a five year-old body, asleep on the ground with an enormous and horrid, purple swelling on her head.

My eternal being was FULL ON in the radiance of the Holy Spirit's immediate Presence, and I was being miraculously Healed. My frontal cranium had been fractured and the C3 vertebra in my neck had been badly compressed with some chipping and both were being Healed. My beloved father was well aware of it by way of the Holy Spirit's messaging through his mind. He told me of this with tearful joy many years later, when he was five years away from passing from his own body.

My wise and discerning spirit being of a father knew very well not to touch my flesh at all but to just keep Praying, Receiving and Radiating the Power of Jesus the Christ, and I Praise God forever as I reflect on his attunement to the vital needs of my body in those moments.

Ten minutes later, I opened my eyes again, still in the same position as when I had first come crashing down from my first attempt at an aerial cartwheel. This time I could see with more focus, although the pain was still very intense.

The first thing I said to my daddy was, "Where is Sarah? Daddy, she is so scared! Go to her and tell her it is not her fault."

He instructed one of my *titas* to take his place while he went off in search of my older sister, Sarah, who had run off to the girls' bathroom in tears and fear. It took daddy awhile to find her, but with the help of some other ladies, she was coaxed out of the bathroom and into his arms. He led her back to me, with tears streaming down her pretty, dark olive-colored face. Her deep brown-black hair was all jumbled with sweat and tears as well. She said nothing but continued to cry.

"It's ok, Sarah. I am all right. Do not worry. Stop crying now."

She stammered, "I thought I had killed you, Elise. I thought you were dead."

At that point I began singing the Catholic song that was most favorite to my sister and me, "Here I am, Lord". It was one that we greatly enjoyed singing together, as the melody and words of it are so precious:

I, the Lord of sea and sky,
I have heard My people cry.
All who dwell in dark and sin,
My hand will save.

I who made the stars of night,
I will make their darkness bright.
Who will bear My light to them?
Whom shall I send?

Here I am Lord, Is it I Lord?
I have heard You calling in the night.
I will go Lord, if You lead me.
I will hold Your people in my heart.

Sarah relaxed and joined in the song as did our other *titos* and *titas* who were nearby. I reached out for her hand and for that of our beloved daddy, and when we had finished the last refrain, I squeezed both of them as tightly as I could, pulling myself up. The extent of the miraculous Healing that God saw fit to administer—and which was impossible for the hand of mankind—was complete for that moment.

It was more than enough. I could turn my head left and right, up and down. I could rotate my shoulders forward and backward, and I got up on my own two feet, to the shock and jubilation of all around.

Daddy thought it was time to leave the party. I think he was right.

The next day, my mother took me to a doctor to have me examined. As my parents were divorced, she was not at the Filipino Christmas party, but had been informed of the accident when daddy brought us back to her house.

She was horrified that I had not been rushed to an ER, as her Faith was nowhere near that of my daddy's. She was greatly upset and concerned for me, and irate at my father for "neglecting" to take me to the hospital.

Well, the medical doctor conducted an MRI of my head, neck and spine, finding only a minor compression to my upper spine. He could verify that there had been trauma to the area. In his review of the MRI, he noticed signs that some of my vertebrae had indeed been broken, but could not discern any present fracture at all.

My mother took the information in disbelief that I had suffered anything more significant than what the doctor could actually see from the imaging.

"Well, Elise, you were lucky to not be dead or turned into a vegetable," she said. She shared the doctor's information with daddy, telling him that there were no serious injuries. But he wisely kept silent about God's Miracle that had actually transpired.

***

BACK TO 2014, BUT IN REMEMBRANCE OF TIMES GONE
The Christmas season of 2014 has just passed, and I am writing here, three days away from my 38th birthday. I take a deep inhale, and I can feel the currents of oxygenated electricity surge up my spine, filling my cranium and exploding in joy unto Heaven. The exhale descends, and still my roots go ever deeper in the reflection of what now IS. God's Healing and Will is my moment-by-moment Reality.

What my body has experienced and what it continues to Receive from God, is directly connected to all that has ever been, all that is, and all that is to come for this world and mankind. What a grand and amazing, simple yet profound GIFT this body is! What a responsibility to the whole of mankind and to all Life, is the personal Healing! What a miracle if and when a person comes to the realization that focus upon one's own Healing is the Healing Prayer for All! *Praise God!*

Yet, I can still feel the tightness of my muscles around my C7 vertebra. Even with my perfect posture, practiced and made a part of my soul's Way for more than 17 years now, the scar tissue within these muscles still speaks to me. I have become a devoted Yogi in these years of rising up in God's Infinite Body of Life, engaging in a daily practice of postures and breathing techniques combined with fervent and ongoing Prayer and a lifestyle of Faith in action. I have spent the past 13 years of my life traveling the Midwest of America, speaking and singing of God's Healing at prisons, hospitals, self-help seminars, business executive retreats, schools, and only recently has the Holy Spirit directed me to present in Christ's Healing ministry at churches. My music has taken on a completely different energy in the last decade, and is presently reaching thousands for the greater choice to be Healed in Christ, but many more still choose to remain in suffering.

There is a major difference between the time necessary to physically Heal, and the time for the mind to be Renewed. The latter can happen instantly but needs moment-by-moment attention to Christ's Mind and not the lies of the past and the stranglehold of negative emotional thinking. The physical Healing is what requires the spirit of Patience, which is a quality of the spiritual warrior.

To live in Faith requires the undoing of all that is of the world of disconnected mankind. To be ALIVE is to breathe our Infinite Lord with every inhale.

The renewal of my mind is ongoing. My spirit is strong, and this sacred Yoga that I treasure is part of God's path for me, and has continued to physically correct the imbalances of my spine and neck over nearly 20 years.

During the period of anorexia, I depleted my own bones of calcium and my body produced toxic ketones as it began to eat itself for survival. At the age of 22, those rickety bones I had created from my own addiction to despair made me feel as if I was 85. When the skeletal system feels hollow and cold, making crunchy sounds all the time, the mind is never at rest. When the body is starved of nutrition, the wailing of stuffed sorrows hold sway.

I must share another miraculous story from that time of self-induced famine. The surging of this story's Healing radiance beckons to spill forth unto all.

***

Famine of the Heart

In 1999 I was 22 years old. My Daddy had died on August 24, 1999, and I was about to physically die for a second time by way of my own doing.

It was a cold and desolate winter that year, not so much because of the heavy snows of this wonderful Missouri land as it was because of my own disconnected heart. After Daddy's passing, my boyfriend and I returned to our rental house in Columbia. He was in school and working a part-time job, and I was feigning being alive, as I was burning calories and my brain away in frenzied exercise and restricted eating.

Really, I cannot call the behavior at that time, "eating." Three designated rice cakes with half a teaspoon of peanut butter per day turned into 3 teaspoon-sized bites of non-fat yogurt a day. I had dropped out of school, had no job, and was supposedly a bride-to-be preparing for marriage in May of 2000.

I told my boyfriend that I thought we should postpone the ceremony for another year, so that I could "catch up on some things." He responded that he wanted me to get some medical and psychiatric help for my condition. I laughed, ignoring his many pleas for me to seek help. There was also a place in my soul that felt hollow in my relationship with him, considering it had been his idea to not get a legal marriage certificate, but to only have a marriage ceremony, with all the fixings and reception to follow. We had been together for about five years by then, but I just blindly accepted his idea, as he seemed confident in his own logic and reasoning of the odd notion.

When his friends would come over, I would disappear into the bedroom, to sit in the dark and listen to them laugh, waiting for something to change. I was waiting for death to consume me easily, effortlessly, while holding on to a thread of hope in this young man's affection for me, and to the precious gleam of my future Children's spirits that tugged at my waning heart. I just assumed he was supposed to be the father who would help bring them forth. But I could not really listen to my heart because it was barely physically beating!

That thread of hope was not strong enough, and I could not allow the mending. Life was desperately attempting to sew me back together, but I was snipping away at the stitches with every bite I refused to eat. The internal demons were winning as I awaited the summer months in anticipation of being able to run the trails again. It was the main excitement that kept me eating something to keep me going.

The twentieth century was ending and the world waited in excitement for the coming of the year 2000. Some people were predicting disasters and the end of the world, while others were spouting assurance of the rise of the Golden Age brought on by Earth's movement within the "photon belt". My boyfriend had faith that I would get over my personal destruction. Little did I know that he was keeping active communication with my stepfather and mother in St. Louis, keeping them abreast of my activities and appearance. They were planning something that I had no clue about, nor did I care to know.

The end of the world did not come, the computers were all still functioning, and I was continuing to lose weight at an alarming rate.

Precious spring emerged and flowed into the tortuously hot summers of mid-Missouri. It was on that one burning morning in July 2000 that I met death. This time, though, I did not cross the threshold.

It was 7:45 a.m. as I prepared to go running on the Missouri Katy Trail, a popular recreational trail winding for many miles across the state of Missouri. Parts of it cut through Columbia, and I could easily access it a few miles from our house. My boyfriend was off to his classes, and I slipped into my sneakers and ran off for my meeting with death.

It is amazing, in retrospect, what the body is capable of, despite physiological and psychological stressors. Soldiers know this best, of course, but when I think about the 96-pound body I had back then, constantly exercising on zero calories, I am baffled in wonderment of how I lasted even that long.

I got a mile and a half into the trail, just away from the noise of the city streets, and surrounded by only the Trees. I loved that "no-zone" blur of light where everything merged together as I pounded my legs into the gravel and only my strained thighs could really be felt. The familiar burn of kinetic force was beginning to feel different on that day, however. My heaving chest and desperate lungs suddenly began to feel like they were about to explode. I kept going and even laughed, doing my best to ignore the fire. But then the burn translated into the sensation of my upper left chest cavity being hit with a demolition ball. I collapsed on the gravel in the throes of a heart attack. I was out and unconscious with no one visible on that part of the trail.

This time there were no sacred realms of light to see. No Voice was there to hear. There was just ... nothing. I was completely unconscious, and I am now aware that my spirit was not at all within my flesh, as the real me had been unable to reside in such a starved cavity of a body. There was nothing I could see outside of that body. I was simply physical, although I was barely even flesh. I was a mass of bones with a thin strip of skin taped to it. The self-induced mental demons had won out. My mind was still too weak, because I had not fully repented of a past I would not let go of ... again.

Or so it seemed in that horrid moment of the worst hell on Earth I had ever brought forth for myself.

When I regained consciousness I was strapped to an IV, with wires stuck to my chest, connected to beeping machines and fluorescent lights all around me. The hospital room I was in had a table with a couple of vases of flowers, a stuffed animal Dog, and a balloon that said, "Get Well Soon." There was one nurse seated beside the bed. She had a surprised look on her face as she pushed a button on the bed's railing.

"Get the doctor. She's awake."

There was a bustle of activity, and a middle-aged man in a white coat came into the room. My boyfriend came in with him.

With a Texas accent, the doctor said, "Hey there, little lady! I'm so glad to see you awake. Rise and shine! You about scared the dickens out of all of us."

I gave a weak smile as he continued, "Now you are not gonna be goin' anywhere for awhile so don't even try to look for those running shoes of yours. If you are ready, I'm gonna come back in an hour and look in on you, ok?"

His smile was so warm, so filled with a power that reminded me of my daddy, although this southern gentleman was a whole lot more alive than my daddy was to me in the state I was in. Still it felt good to see his face, first thing. I was grateful for this doctor, whom I recognized as the Student Health doctor from the university I had attended. I had seen him a few months prior, at the one doctor's visit I had agreed to, per my family's request. He had expressed concern for the serious danger posed by my lack of body fat, my suffering heart, and my loss of hearing due to the Eustachian tubes being stripped of fat, but it had gone in one ear and out the other finding nothing in between.

When he came back an hour later, I was much more alert, as they had been pumping glucose into my body. I felt jittery and cold and was shaking. The nurse brought in 3 extra blankets, bundling me up in that air-conditioned building as 100+ degree temperatures raged outside.

The doctor explained to me, in the presence of my worried boyfriend, that my parents were on their way to Columbia, and that I had indeed had a heart attack.

He said, "You are blessed beyond my comprehension, Elise. I am aware of your recent medical history from a few years back, dear. A gentleman found you slumped on the MKT, picked you up, and ran you back into town, straight to Student Health. He did not have a phone, but he carried you all the way to our office. We called an EMT and here you are. By the Grace of God, here you are."

"Who was the man? What was his name?" I asked feebly.

"The only thing he said when he carried you into Student Health, was 'My name is Michael, and I found this young girl laying on the trail. I do not think she is fully dead, but she is close. Take care of her.' Then he walked out the door. The staff was in such a frenzy over you, that no one followed him out to find out more about him."

Streams of God's Holy Light made manifest through the form of an angel; that is who he was. I never found out more about that man, nor will I in this lifetime, but I sure do know Who was filling him and Who sent him to rescue that body of mine! *Praise God!*

***

Regarding the Hatred of the World for That Which Is Pure

I am going to digress here slightly, because there is something supernaturally important that must be expressed regarding the gift of Miracles made manifest through an individual. I have been sharing rays of God's Truth, and the true stories of my little lifetime on this planet, because I live on FIRE with God's Will for the perfection of your own experience down here, so that you may choose Christ over and beyond the world, as the substance of your life. What I am about to say is so blazingly spot-on, that I will become further hated by many because of it. The following may be tough for some of you to chew on, and if, instead, you feel His Breath of fresh air and a rekindled flame in your heart, then PRAISE GOD!

I bless you all in the Name of Jesus the Christ.

One becomes ABNORMAL to the world, to individuals, and even to popular Christianity when Miracles consume the formerly personal life.

There is no such thing as the personal life, once Jesus' Grip takes hold, for the whole of ALL Life belongs to God Almighty, His Son Jesus Christ and the Holy Spirit, as ONE BODY.

When a person has been so washed through, so utterly transformed by the Living Fire of Christ, so that every single moment of the life is ALIGHT in the JOY of living His Will ... Well, this is a fire that the world cannot lay eyes upon nor accept, because the widespread dispensation of the Holy Spirit's massive Healings is no longer upon Earth as it once was in the days of the great Christian evangelists such as John G. Lake, William Branham, and Kathryn Kuhlman. In those days, thousands of people Received powerful and permanent spiritual and physical healings en masse. But Kathryn Kuhlman's ministry was the last of the great dispensations of the Holy Spirit, and there will never be another.

People get jealous of the few individuals nowadays who really do Receive something powerful from God Almighty. They do not have it for themselves, and their soulful yearning might be honest and good at first, but then it turns to a certain kind of spiritual lusting when they observe that they never receive what they will forth in Prayer—although they would never admit that it is a form of lust. The negative emotions of ego are a beast even among the religious of this world, who then create false faces of spiritualized ego while claiming sanctified knowledge of God's Word. In many ways, this is worse than the ego lusts of materialism, sexual perversion, vanity, and greed. And Christian churches of the 21st century are rife with individuals who have made this kind of face out of their own identity, blaspheming the very purity of Jesus the Christ by claiming His Righteousness as the cornerstone of their judgments and attitudes. Have a look at private Facebook Christian groups, especially those describing themselves as "discussion" pages, and you will get a good dose of false-face spiritual ego, front and center. If you join one, I recommend that you do so from a healthy distance, using great discernment always.

If you call yourself "Christian", you must, in every way, point the finger at your own disconnected and dis-eased mind, commanding its Renewal in Christ in every single moment, no matter how long you are alive in a body on Earth. To be a True Christian is an ongoing devotional relationship in progress, and it requires the will of a quiet, peaceful warrior who is determined to embody the Heart and Mind of the Only God Who is the Way, the Truth, and the Life. You are here to Know GOD and to radiate His Will, so that His Works come through your life for the benefit of others, and so that YOU can radiate Heaven on Earth.

It is a simple and private relationship that MIGHT be called to expand so as to join others in the community of a church or spiritual family. But it is NOT a requirement to do so.

Hear me clearly: The ESSENCE of the Church is the Spirit of Jesus Christ, and no man's mind or religion can lay claim to it.

Where two people are gathered, in Jesus' Name, so there He is. That is the Simplicity and perfection that Jesus wanted the Apostles to understand and to teach. Jesus knew that because of the degree of evil and disconnection that held sway in the collective mind of mankind, a camaraderie and a community in Truth was necessary for the people who would choose Christ. It was for that purpose that the 12 most trained and ready of the original disciples were called to the task of bringing it forth. This was no easy job in the world of Jesus' time, where evil was codified in the political and social order, but they carried forth, touching thousands. Since that time their work has been mutated by man's continued self-centeredness of mankind, bringing forth the dogmas, separation, and rigidities of the various churches upon planet Earth.

The Essence of the Church was and IS this: to reach out to one another in the Love of God, to break the Holy Bread together in shared meals, and to support one another in the Way of Christ, regularly, so as to then radiate a pure Life in His Body. It was and is as simple as that.

This is not, however, what is made manifest through every mind of all those who call themselves "Christian", nor is it apparent in the majority of churches on Earth today. If you are a true Christian, then you should KNOW that you are not bound to ANYTHING that is evil or negative in nature. You have been cleansed of it permanently and completely, so do your best not to act as if it still plagues you. Get it OUT of you, moment by moment!

If you really love Jesus, then your life should be an ongoing path of discovery in how to LOVE Him more in the way you speak, work, act, feel, think, eat, live, and relate to others. No matter what happens to you in your life, if you are one who is REALLY devoted to the Will of God, you will forge ahead, moment by moment, choosing the activity or making the decision which is born of your contemplation and Prayer unto Jesus the Christ's direction. If you really are a radiant Christian, confident in Christ, you would never dare to judge anyone, especially another Christian. If you do not like another person's walk or talk, that is perfectly acceptable. Move along. They have no bearing upon your communion in Christ. If you are called by the Holy Spirit to speak out against obvious evil and wrongdoing, then so be it. Do so in the Purity and Muscle of the Sword of Peace which only Jesus the Christ is. Leave yourself out of it. It's not about you. There is only God Almighty's Will and nothing more to be done through you but this.

How many churches widely profess and practice the Will of God's Healing? Where is the charismatic energy of JOY in the profession that Jesus has completely wiped away the bonds of sin, disease and death? How many church communities in this world really radiate this Truthful Joy, translating it into organized social action and political change? Sure, there are many hugely wealthy churches out there who gather on Sundays with their loud worship music, replete with drum kits, electric guitars, loudspeakers and stage lights, but I tell you, this is NOT charismatic Joy of Jesus the Christ. This is another face of the world's manifested collective ego posing as religious and spiritual fervor.

Jesus stole away from the crowds to Pray.

He avoided them after he multiplied the loaves and fishes, and after he gave the Sermon on the Mount. He told the disciples that the best Prayer was given in the darkness of a closet, with no adornment and no fancy words. He told those whom He Healed to speak not of Himself as being the one Who had healed them, but to give all the Praise and Glory to ELOI, to the ONE Father in Heaven. Did they do this? Very few. Their egos got all excited and their little mouths blabbered to everyone, doing exactly what Jesus told them NOT to say and do. And the crowds kept on coming for Him. And He always gave them what they sought, but only if it was aligned with the Will of the ONE.

One who has been graced with the impossible made manifest in the form of physical Miracles becomes the black sheep even to many who say they know and love the WORD of God in religious faith. There are many so-called "Christians" who immediately try to defame the testimony of one who professes his or her amazing healing story as not bound to Jesus' Name, and who further degrade the one who then goes out into the world to bear WITNESS to what has been received. They publicly slander the individual, questioning the person's authenticity in Christ, the veracity of the Miracle story, they attempt to block or stop any ministry that individual is bringing forth. This is nothing more than the work of a dead devil's minions wearing the masks of "Christians." This reality is so contrary to what SHOULD happen via individuals through established religion. I state clearly that I am not charging all church-going Christians with such behavior, but those whom I describe are prevalent, and I bear first-hand experience with their dark energies towards myself.

The fact that each and every Christian church (no matter what the branch or denomination of Christianity) is NOT collectively behaving like a mini-"Samaritan's Purse," (which is a direct Christ-centered organization that serves those who are suffering the whole world round) nor imitating the Billy Graham Organization (whose leader has brought millions back to Christ's Love) is a travesty. The heart of Christ as chosen by millions if not billions of Christians should be having a direct effect on local, state, and federal governments because the Mind of Christ is put into the activity of Unconditional Love in all aspects of life in the social order. But it is NOT this way, and it is a shame and a grievance to Jesus the Christ, our ONE God Almighty.

On the microcosmic level, when so-called Christians denounce or call into question the pure testimony of a Miracle through the individual life of another, it is the same as stabbing Jesus in the side, all over again. I have had a few "Christians" tell me that I was brought back from the dead by the devil, because my testimony also discusses at length, the Supernatural and mystical aspects of what Lives Beyond. I have been called a "midwife of satan" because I have co-authored the most powerful Trilogy of books on the planet: a Christian allegory that uses secular and fantastical words to metaphorically describe what living in the Holy Spirit looks like on Earth through REAL people. To reach out to an atheistic and "secular" world, using imagery that such people can accept and understand, while writing of GOD's TRUTH, is exactly what Christ did in his teaching via parables. It is what WORKS. But apparently, when some learned that I used to be a practicing traditional lay midwife for home birthing mothers, coupled with the fact that the first book of our allegorical Trilogy is entitled The Strong Witch Society, some "Christians" out there not only armed themselves with stones, but also started to build their pyres in preparation for me.

I have learned by way of my ministry that the more these types of false faces try to spit their venom, the brighter and more focused my Fire for Christ's Healing burns. It's not me they are hurting; it is our Beloved Lord they are despising.

Blessed are the Meek. It is the simple ones, some of whom have never even read the Bible, who are often used to bring forth God's Lightning Miracles. I have met the most amazing men and women blessed by God's Hand and LIVING it, in my traveling ministry, who were totally unlettered in Christian theology. A few of whom could not even read, yet were more godly than any of the most prestigious Christian ministers, priests, or evangelists.

When there is just one person who seeks ways to belittle another's Miracle made manifest, they are HURTING the WHOLE of God's Life and destroying God's Grip on their own lives.

There is a major difference between asking questions of one who professes God's Miracles in an honest effort to understand and to necessarily test the spirit, as contrasted with an illegitimate branding of one who speaks of God's Hand working through his or her life. Surely it is natural to be curious about a person's story, and reasonable questions of the specifics should and must be asked. For a Miracle is just that—A MIRACLE! And because Miracles are Divinely born and supernatural, the details astound and bewilder one who has not experienced anything of the like. Seek to understand with a purified heart, ask questions from this state of mind, and the power of Christ's radiance will saturate you, by way of the Miraculous story shared.

***

God's Supernatural HUM and My Early Years in This Lifetime

I am rewinding a bit here to describe how it was for me in the beginning of this little lifetime when, as a very young child, my spirit consciousness was kept strong for the most part. Even then, amidst the chaos of my biological mother and father, I knew I was not of this world, and that my family on Earth was not my TRUE family. This knowing was maintained with great force for a good many years. However, as the child remains in that kind of environment it is so bombarded by the ego-isms of other adults that maintaining its spiritual knowing and growing up CHOOSING to Return to God's Truth becomes the ultimate challenge of a lifetime.

By bringing forth the impossible in the Miracles of my life, Christ gave me complete attunement and reminded me of what it is that I am here on Earth to accomplish for His Plan, and of what I have known for far longer than this lifetime. It is all for the benefit of life on Earth and beyond, and I give All Praise and Glory, always, unto our One Lord and King.

Those of you who have met me by way of The Diary of Mary Bliss Parsons, volumes 1,2, & 3, (co-authored with D H Parsons) will be aware that I am Gifted with what is termed, the "HUM." It is a part of who I am as spirit. In this section, I will go into some detail about the HUM and how I was aware of it even from infancy.

The Miracles that have transpired through my Earthly body and soul, and which are further described in this book are exclusively because of and maintained by the Mercy of God Almighty and His Hand and Will alone through Jesus Christ.

There is an aspect of Truth, which this world will never be able to collectively grasp because it is beyond the scope of mankind's disconnected mindscape. You, however, as spirit individuals open enough to be reading this book, have the obvious capability to possibly understand.

God is Divinely Supernatural. God's Living Body is unseen, ceaseless, and Indomitable in His exclusive Might and Glory. His Divine Son, Jesus Christ is the Second Person of His Being, having been sent of the Body of the ONE God, to Earth, so that all who are chosen, would Return to Him. His Spirit is what was made available to His adopted children, after the Christ Returned to Heaven. This THREE PERSONS IN ONE is forever, our ONE God Almighty. So now, let me explain to you how the Holy Spirit moves through with Healing, as I explain to you my connection within the HUM from childhood, and beyond time.

THE DESCRIPTION OF GOD'S SUPERNATURAL REALITY CONTINUES

The HUM of God Almighty is a Force, a Ray of His Power that can nourish and create, supernaturally and naturally heal and rejuvenate, as well as destroy and demolish that which needs to be removed, according to God's Great Plan. The HUM is the vibratory energy by which God's Creation Frequency is fueled.

The Creation Frequency is God's patterned network of LIFE, the blueprint of cosmic energy that composes all things and beings within all universes, galaxies, and solar systems. It is the invisible Perfection of light structure that keeps everything together in form: suns, stars, planets, comets, trees, skies, soils, people, rocks, the magnetic core of this Earth, animals, and on and on. If one were capable of seeing it—and no human being on planet Earth is—it would look like trillions upon trillions of filaments of light, woven together and crisscrossing to make an intricate Web, studded with various forms of condensed light defining all those things that fill the universes. God's Creation Frequency gives rise to and sustains all sentient and non-sentient beings by means of the cosmic light. To view this Web of Life would indeed be blinding.

The Source of the HUM is God alone. It is used and directed with specific focus and purpose, according to the needs of any beings or civilizations, throughout the many universes of God's enormous Body of Life.

Communion with the HUM is one of my eternal Gifts. In this particular life as the soul-mind identity of Elise R. Brion, I have used it in Awareness since infancy, primarily to radiate Christ's Healing, the major focus of God's Will for this time and space in the story of mankind on Earth.

Now, when I say HUM, I do not simply refer to the vibration anyone can make when the lips are kept together and breath is sent across the vocal cords with intention. Remember, I explained that the HUM is the Supernatural wavelength by which the Holy Spirit sends necessary Healing energy for this dimension where Earth resides.

For visualization, picture the rays of an enormous galactic sun singularly directed by Christ's Heart, sent forth in a laser-like focused concentration, entering the solar system where Earth resides. God uses specific beings for specific purposes throughout the history of mankind on Earth. My assignment from ELOI, (Who IS God) which has been the same for millions of years, is to be His messenger, His transmitter to embody and radiate this exact HUM of God Almighty's Healing.

When I was an infant, my family noticed that a buzzing sound came from my body, and was frequently noticeable. My father found it strange at first, and no one could figure out a physiological reason for it, even after taking my little infant body to a pediatrician who could hear it as well. After awhile, the standing joke of the Filipino side of my family was that "Elise is the Queen Bee."

As I grew into childhood, I would put the HUM into focused use when my father had common ailments: head colds, insomnia, indigestion, and over-eating, a behavior that would eventually lead to his congestive heart failure. My earliest memory of using the HUM on him was when I was three years old. My father had a personal habit of "eating away a cold" with bountiful extra helpings of white rice, fried fish, *pancit* (a Filipino noodle dish), and flan for dessert. He believed that his body needed extra energy to strengthen his white blood cells. At the dining table, one evening, as he sneezed incessantly over his now empty second plate of food, and was reaching for more, I put the HUM upon him. With my little hands extended under the glass table top obscured by placemats so no one could see, I stretched out my fingers as wide as I could, and I just stared at my daddy's face. This was the first experience of the HUM turning into something more audible by way of my own control. I translated the surging Force of what can best be described as a searing Silver-Blue color into a vibratory sound emanating from the whole of my little three-year-old body. I sent the current—so natural for me to see and feel all the time, a current that I experienced as a huge electric-like bubble all around me constantly, a current which was the normal reality for me—into the very body of my beloved daddy so he would "wake up."

As I said, that moment in my childhood was the first time I consciously directed the HUM with my own will. The sound was now audible to ears that were listening, but the frequency of the HUM was known only to myself. The very moment I did it, my daddy about fell over backwards in his chair. Really.

My three-year old soulful intention was simply to make him "wake up", which in that moment meant to stop eating so much. Coincidingly, I was directing the Rays of Jesus Christ's Healing into my daddy's flesh with the current of light that God was making known to my perception, the Silver-Blue, as a means of immediately clearing the virus that was challenging his immune system. I had not expected him to physically jolt backwards like that, nor was that a part of my focus, but at the age of three years, the co-habitation of my spirit with my soul and flesh was very strong. He caught himself before falling, looked all around at the family sitting at the table and said, "Was there an earthquake that just hit?"

"No, Lilli," my *tita* replied.

"What in God's Name was that, then?" he said, truly perplexed.

"Maybe it was your sneezes," said my *lola* (grandma).

"I was not sneezing when it happened, but all of a sudden, I do not feel congested or achy at all. All of that sickness is just gone!"

"Ok, then why question what it was, Lilli?" said my first *tita*.

"*Blesses sa akin ng Dios*," my father replied, making the Sign of the Cross upon his face and chest. "God blesses me," Then he added, "You know, I do not want any more food. I am finished."

Nobody had had their eye on my little arms outstretched under the see-through glass table with placemats. Nobody was paying attention to the audible hum that was streaming from my body, and CERTAINLY none of my sweet little Filipino family could see what was shooting through the whole of my toddler self, saturating my daddy and them all, in Christ's Truth.

I quickly came to realize that my daddy had many more problems than just occasional head colds and overeating. He was an overworked medical doctor, a psychiatrist with an incredible load of clients to see in his office, and rounds to make at the three hospitals he also worked for. But it was his stuffed up rage and hurt which would most challenge my HUM in the next 10 years of this little Earthly life.

What is most important is the nature of the spiritual innocence of a child, and how it is abused and destroyed by all ego-isms of adults, who are the microcosm of this world.

A child is not innocent just because it has not been exposed to the vile ways of the world. When a child is in utero, it is still being interfused with the Divine's supernatural rays of the HUM of Christ, giving spiritual influence to the very formation of the fleshly temple to be used for God's Will. The tiny embryo is fed with spiritual instruction—the cosmic nourishment that streams from God's Great Tree of Life.

A child's spirit is told by Christ what family it is being born to, what general mission within God's Great Plan it has been assigned to work, and what specific aspects of God's Will it is to emanate to the adults in that family and to the world at large. This is all crystal clear in the spirit mind, but then it must sink down into the slow-moving third dimensional realm where Earth is located. The spirit being becomes encapsulated and reduced in cosmic strength, limited to the body cavity of a totally incapable child, whose nervous system is contained and formed by the parameters of human physiology and the pitiful disconnections of man's mental realm.

This is comparable to a crewman on a supply Mother Ship carrying important goods. The Captain tells the crewman that the only way to reach those who need the goods is to jump off the ship into unknown waters, swim to reach the shore, then hand over the goods for the benefit of those who live there. The trouble is, that the one who agrees to be the carrier of the goods has no ability to see what lives in those waters, how long it will take for the goods to be safely delivered, and whether or not the people who live there will be accepting of the goods from the Mother Ship that the crewman has to offer.

So here is a spirit being now ready to enter into the world after a 9-month gestation period, subjected and exposed to the varying degrees of physical, emotional, mental, and spiritual health of the biological mother (who is not the spiritual mother of the being). These factors, whether they be positive or negative immediately affect the degree to which the spirit being is able to remain in the body capsule of the child. Depending on the peace or chaos of the physical labor and delivery, as well as the aforementioned factors, a spirit being is faced with a multitude of unknown influences and oppressive forces from the very moment the sperm hits the egg.

Now, take a moment to think about the realm of people on Earth into which a child is born, with all of the individual and collective ego-isms of cultural restrictions, spiritual and soulful immaturity, war and all its hellish qualities, physical and social iniquities, material and physically bound mindsets, and overall distractions from God. All of these and more contribute to the formation of the soul (which is a child's learned mind), while distancing and disconnecting the child from its original Awareness of being a spirit, that of belonging to God's Will first and foremost. Oh, what hell a spirit coming to Earth is born to! The task of returning one person to Christ is huge, and the work of exorcism necessary to bring about the Re-discovery of one's true origin as a spirit being seems nearly impossible.

HUMMING CHRIST'S HEALING INTO THIS WORLD

Even before the experience as a three year old at the dinner table with my *tai*, my daddy, I was aware of the HUM coming through me. My daddy took me out into the gardens frequently as a baby, and there I saw the buzzing energy of the Rose bushes against the house, the way the stoic Tree trunks so majestically held their vibratory light together in beautiful form, and the playful dance of Green crystal-like waves of the grass.

Animals were a sheer and wondrous delight for me. When I was older, my father told me of how I would shriek for joy when I saw a squirrel, a dog, a cat, a bird, and then of making "odd cadences with your lips, like you were speaking to them in another language that did not exist on Earth." He said that when I made these sounds, oftentimes the animal would stop what it was doing, turn in our direction, and make an effort to come closer to where I was.

When I was five years old, I had a habit of slipping out the back door while no one was looking, just to go sit in the backyard to wait for one of my little friends to come join me. I was not waiting for a neighborhood playmate, but for a butterfly, a caterpillar, a worm, a leisurely cat, some dog, or bird. I always just sat in the same spot, making my sounds (both internally and externally) in order to call out to them. Always, some sacred spirit being creature made its way to me. I never spoke to it with words, but with the HUM. This communication was not always in direct picture images in my little mind, but within the HUM, which is entirely different.

It is commonly said in the discussion of telepathy and remote viewing that thinking in pictures is the core of these extra-sensory abilities. This is quite true with regards to what I mean concerning talking within the HUM.

Again, the HUM is a Ray of God's Indomitable Force, a collective beam of His divine Energy having a myriad of functional purposes and uses throughout all dimensions. The rays of Christ's Healing, destruction, creative energy, and more are all aspects of the HUM. My assignment from the early years to this present moment was and continues to be to use the HUM to focus Christ's Nourishment, Nurturing, and Healing on Earth. So, when I would just sit upon the grass, I knew I was becoming that grass in that moment, joining completely with the spirit of the grass in full, so that I could then become connected with another creature spirit being as a part of Christ's Healing. You see, at that tender age, I was already beginning to see my father explode in his raging episodes, and I used the daily practice of BECOMING with my nature friends as a means of Christ's Healing of the negativity my Earth family was bringing forth.

Let me share a picture with you of my daddy's sweetness, of his soul and spirit's harmonic resonance within the HUM. These moments are my most cherished memories of when I KNEW he was happiest in his life, for I could see the light of his being and all that emanated from his heart.

My daddy taught me the beauty of music by way of his passion for it. He would perch my little body on the piano bench next to him when he would play his beloved original compositions, and he would just sing his heart out! I learned how to control my breath in vibrato singing, by way of his instruction. I learned how his own self-taught piano mastery was something that I could imitate. Unlike his adoration for piano and his singing voice, my passion was my VOICE.

I was about four years old when I began to accompany him in duets, and together we filled that house in south St. Louis with everything from songs of Les Miserables to Verdi to Abba. My daddy loved music and so did I. Oh, the COLORS we brought forth through our joy of making music together! It was just so much fun to have my daddy in song. Not yet aware of the gigantic spirit contained in my little body, he brought forth a chunk of heaven for myself and for the whole of the world by way of his love for me through his music.

When I was even younger, I would crawl under the piano, only to fall asleep to the humming nourishment of the piano's reverberating body as my daddy danced his fingers along the keys. I really believed that God was guiding him to use his voice and piano playing as a way of being Healed, and I had full Faith that my daddy would one day be able to see the HUM and use it the way I could. That, of course, was an innocent longing, a need I had to offset the feelings of loneliness I had, knowing that he was the one member of my Earth family who could possibly come to remember himself as a spirit being and not just as a man.

But he did use his music as a form of soulful and spiritual medicine. He knew so many Filipino folk songs and classical pieces by heart, and after a long and tiresome day of being a psychiatrist, and after one of his heavy Filipino dinners, he would let it all out in the music room. I Prayed to Christ as a young child that his passion for expression in music would be enough to get him through the layers of demonic negative emotions he had so deeply stuffed inside.

At first, I was never scared of my daddy's emotional explosions, because they were simply foreign to me in energy. They did not compute. So I could just observe him with a sort of objectivity when he was screaming at the top of his lungs and throwing things against the walls. This is a clear example of how my spirit was dominant in that little body of mine, for emotional negativity is a foreign thing to a spirit being who knows it belongs to Christ.

But I just KNEW these explosions were not right at all, because of what I could see and feel when his body would turn ugly colors and his light pattern would become totally chaotic and out of form. He could go from having just played beautiful music for hours, with oceanic rainbow light swirling from the whole of his body, to a disjointed ugly mass of Grey-Brown-Green colors the moment his rages took hold. I knew he needed my help, and I knew how to stream it to him by way of my belonging to the HUM of God Almighty.

The inhabitants of this world would be wise to retrain the mind to perceive what science has already proven: the essence of Life as light. For most of Earth's residents this perceptive ability will never come as truly natural, but people would be smart to practice the visualization of objects as collections of light as a part of their Renewal and Healing in Christ, using the internet to find artistic depictions of the Great Tree of Life for example, or the meridian light structure of the human form as another, to help the mind to see beyond materiality and into the

Heart of Christ. This practice is actually a part of God's Will to live the Kingdom.

I have already described a bit of how the HUM is a Force of God's Power, emanating energies of creation, destruction, and Healing of Christ, and it is not a Force that can be willed forth by ANYBODY in form on Earth (with the exception, of course, of Jesus the Christ). The HUM is a Force that takes over only when God wants it to, and when I say it streamed through me to my dear daddy, I mean what I say.

Sometimes the Healing Rays of the HUM would gently flow through my body in calm waves of crystal Blue-Silver, sometimes in the form of harmonic Green melodies that only I could hear, and other times Orange-Pink lightning streaks would zap through me in the wee hours of the morning. When I was around eight years old, I realized that I was being awakened every morning at three AM exactly, when the Orange-Pink "zappers" would come through.

It wasn't that I could not understand what the supernatural Rays were about. Every time a flood of them became more focused, more forceful, and with something other than their usual Navy Blue waving bubble (for that's how the HUM appeared to me in its "neutral state" in a calmed or "waiting" mode) my little mind was crystal clear about whom specifically that particular woosh of the HUM was to be directed. The image of that person or place or thing would be very clear in my mind, and all I did was stay focused upon him, her, it, or the place on Earth.

By all normative social standards as this world thinks and operates, if I had tried to explain to anybody what my supernatural perceptions and reality looked like, I would have been drugged up and put under lock and key in a heartbeat. But I never threw my pearls before swine, and I knew that what came through me was something that had to be protected so that I could continue to be connected within it. The HUM remained my precious secret for a good long while.

And I was my daddy's precious little girl.

I was most assuredly my daddy's favored child, and that was perfectly fine by me, at first. Even though his expressed affection for my older sister and myself was to become very imbalanced, I loved being the apple of his eye.

In those happy moments with daddy, I learned to stretch out the positive frequencies he emanated from his joyous heart, energetically stretching them with the HUM because I was melding them into the world at large. It was an easy thing for me to see and do. I used my spirit gaze to spread the Golden and Orange rays of his laughter and songs across the whole of this Earth and beyond. I wove them back into this world's dimension, enveloping my daddy with his own joy augmented by the HUM and the Love of Christ. I knew this was enough to keep him happy and healthy for the very long and fulfilling Earth time that he was meant to experience here. Besides that, he was my daddy, and I wanted him to remain as such. It worked with precision for a while, and then the stuffed evil energy began to emerge from his mind, and the battle began.

***

A Prayer in Conviction of
Christ's Healing Fire

Through this re-telling of the next wave of my Childhood, I radiate an oceanic wave of Crystal Silver Blue Fire upon this world, engulfing and saturating each and every Child, each and every being whose purity has been maligned. I sweep you all up within my inhaling heart in the Living Firelight of Jesus the Christ. In His precious and Holy Name, you are all cleansed and nourished in this indomitable Love.

Now I BREATHE FORTH my story for the instant rejuvenation of those yearning to be free of a past which seems to haunt the psyches and souls of humanity, the whole world round.

***

Stuffed rage, depression, and sorrow can only lay dormant for so long, when, as with a sleeping volcano, there comes a moment when the burn of what has been trained to sleep comes roaring out of the depths of a person's soul-mind with an evil fire, threatening the innocence and the purity of a wee one in that person's care.

I say to all the children of Earth, I truly do wrap my spirit around you. What has been and is being done to you has no power in the Breath with which I envelope the whole of this world ... right now.

I want you, the reader, to focus upon your own Breath with loving attention right now—such a dear and perfect inhale. For He truly has already Healed you in full, and now it is you who must fully come to embody this Truth in welcoming, acceptance, and CONVICTION, not just for your own soul's Healing, but for the Healing of all who are weakened and vulnerable on this planet. The energies of the CHRIST must be embodied now.

***

How Evil Attempted to Sever My Soul from Spirit

One of the greatest ironies of life as a human being is that even within the chaos and disharmony of being raised in disconnection from God Almighty, there can still be the embodiment of loving nurturance and goodwill for a child and for all beings on Earth. The Sun always sheds its rays upon one who is abused, neglected, and mal-nourished; the rain always saturates the Earth; the seasons always bring renewal of Nature for all who live within its bounty of Grace from God.

It is strong in my Awareness that no matter what, a person can find many examples of the Indomitable Love that God Almighty makes manifest for the personal life, so that when it comes right down to the bare Truth of the matter, no thing, no person, no trauma of the past has any bearing on the Infinite Reality of God's Timeless Love and Providence for all beings, and beyond time.

I write the following sections in respectful dedication to and about my mother and my other dad, who is my stepfather, in an attempt to summarize their contribution to my life, highlighting the struggles of their parenthood of me, and the joys of their unique influence upon my soul in my love for all humanity. While I wish to honor them both, I must also candidly relate what happens to the spirit-Awareness of a child when there are parents who do not believe in Jesus the Christ as the only Savior, Redeemer, and Healer, as One in God Almighty. The telling of this story requires that I share some personal details about what happened to my mind as I grew up in the custody and care of ones who had come to reject the Truth of Christ as Lord above and for All. For what happened to my mind directly—but temporarily, Praise God—affected my attunement and connection to my own eternal and powerful spirit in a dangerous fashion. The story of these two and that of my biological daddy intertwine.

My Earth mother and step-dad are still alive today. They will always hold a dear place in my heart, because of who they are as individuals, as my Earth parents, and because of their own roles within God's Great Plan.

Contrary to Filipino custom and culture, where human marriage was meant to be for life, my biological father and mother divorced when I was eight months old. It was my American-born Caucasian mother who asked for the divorce, and understandably so. By the time of the birth of her second child, she was experiencing with increasing frequency the emotionally psychotic episodes of my dad. With my four-year old sister and this newborn baby girl, she was burdened by grave responsibilities and the need to maintain personal sanity within her life at that time.

Given the mysteries of my daddy's behavior, and the unpredictability of the emotional explosions in the last few years of their marriage, it is a wonder that my mother also decided to put herself through law school while pregnant with me. Interestingly, a major concern for her was that she would go into labor during her finals week. I am, however, a good listener, and I was born a few days after she had taken all of her exams, which she passed with flying colors!

She was a Caucasian woman, married to an Asian man in the 60s and 70s, with one small child and an infant, and working hard to become an attorney. Although her university degrees and promising professional career conferred her with a level of privilege, she had come from a small Kentucky town where her mother was a homemaker and her father worked in a steel mill.

Growing up with three other siblings in a devout Roman Catholic household, my mother was baptized, raised, and educated within the Christian Faith. Her parents were hard working individuals with their own childhood stories rife with physical hardship and material deprivation. My mother's parents embodied Christ's Way in their selflessness and dedication to family and to human beings in general. At a time when it was not a popular thing to be vocal about racial issues, my grandmother and grandfather walked the walk of being Christian when encountering racist behaviors and thinking from other White people in their community. Although they were not involved in organized social justice groups, they instilled in my own mother, by the Way of Christ's Teachings, the importance of treating all people with equal respect, no matter the look of the surface of the flesh.

But starting in college, my mom began to question the ways of the world, not with the lens of Christ, but through the lens of mankind's ideation as she became interested in issues of social justice and feminism. She left her small-town Kentucky days behind her and moved to the big city of St. Louis to study social work at St. Louis University. She met my father when she was a social worker and he was employed as a medical intern. Ironically—in view of what their life story would look like in just a few more years—they met in the psychiatric institution where they were both working on staff.

My mother was 32 years old when she gave birth to me. My earliest memory of her is a vivid image of a tall woman with curly brunette hair and a smile bigger than her face. She was the one who could do no wrong, the one who was safe, when I was a child. She was the one who read to my sister and me every night from books from the local library. She was the one into whose bed I loved to slip, from toddlerhood to five years of age, after she had tucked me into my own bed in my own bedroom with a "Good night, I love you. Sweet dreams," sealed with a kiss on the forehead. This was the nightly ritual that I had known, and it was an emotional bedrock for my little being. There was something immediately cleansing about the ritual of storybooks, tuck in, and the nighttime blessing, although there was not a word of Worship unto God in direct verbalization. It truly was the Rays of the Holy Spirit coming through my mother, uniting with my little soul and the core essence of my spirit. This ritual was an earthly lifeline providing an anchor for me and my older sister.

My sweet mom kept all stories of my daddy's earlier psychotic behavior in the secret of her heart for so many years, and it was she who received me as my own response to his behavior escalated from neutral, to frightened, to terrified. Even so, she was not the one to insist and ensure that by way of Jesus Christ, the evil be cast from the lives of my sister and me, and from her own.

By that time in her life, my mother had stopped going to church, and stopped believing in Christ as the only Redeemer and Savior. I speculate that this was the result of not just her choice to embrace the social ideologies of the world, but that the effect of having to deal with my father also contributed to her falling away from the Lord. A mind that chooses to see life on Earth with the mind of mankind, as opposed to the Truth of God, and has experienced trauma or abuse is indeed challenged in Faith.

I wonder about this even now, with this story done and so long gone in the ashes of time. Even if she had remained a Christian, would this have been enough to carry her through, considering that her mind was so filled with the disconnected and limited views of worldly social inequality and feminism, which inherently reject God's Truth? Both ideologies, while correctly focusing on the oppression of mankind as caused by mankind itself, fail to make the connection that all iniquity stems from the actions of a collective species that does not accept that it belongs to God Almighty. In the eternal Truth of this Holy Communion, iniquity and suffering, oppression and worldly domination are impossibilities.

Among other things, the feminism of the 70s espoused that Christianity was a sexist religion, so my mother analyzed all situations focused upon inequities between races, inequities due to economics, and inequities due to sexism and chauvinism. There were the "haves" and the "have-nots", the privileged and the oppressed, and the institutionalized roles of men and women in a sexist world. Jesus Christ had no place in her soul mind, nor in her body and heart because "God was just a man" and nothing but, in her analysis of Christianity. Gone were the days of her innocent Faith in the Holy WORD, which her own mother and father had so dutifully tried to embody for their children.

Also, she could not see my father's anger as the result of the evils of the sin that it was, so she had completely rejected Christ's Presence as the only Power that could protect her and her children. She did not reflect on his own insane and horrifying childhood, of witnessing warfare as a part of every moment of his childhood in the Philippine islands, as the root of his hellish emotional explosions.

As a result of this blindness, she made her soul and heart subject to the emotional drama of it all, and when she felt us old enough to understand the words she used, she did not hold back in explaining exactly what her mental analysis had so concluded. She saw his psychotic behavior strictly according to the lens of her university psychology training—that he suffered from a chronic depression turned into a unique kind of lunacy. Starting when I was around six years old, I began to hear how ironic it was that in her opinion my daddy was a psychiatrist who should be treated by a psychiatrist, and on and on.

She was frightened of him both energetically and practically, and with good reason.

Interestingly, both my mother and my father found another life mate around the same space of time, and each married their new spouse within months of each other.

I was six years old.

What my mother had good reason to fear was the fact that my father started to take her to court. He had discovered that there was another man; my soon-to-be stepfather—whom I shall occasionally refer to as "step-dad" for point of reference, but whom I more regularly call "dad", as that is who he is to me—who had actually moved into our house.

Admittedly, my mother's courtship with my step-dad was lightning fire quick, and was followed by an even quicker move-in. They were now living together in the house that my father and mother had purchased some 10 years prior, and to which my father still held the mortgage. Thus began the first of many court battles.

At first the court litigation was just between the two of them, over the house. My father hated it that there was another man living in the home he had bought, and that this man would have an influence on his own Children, so he made certain things financially complicated for my mother because of it.

But my daddy always dutifully paid her a hefty amount of child support, keeping a keen eye on my sister and me. As angry as he was toward my mother, he was always a 100% provider for us. This fact, in contrast to all of the rest of the chaos of his life, shows the core strength of my father's character, as well as the core of his soul. I knew then, and even stronger now, how much he truly loved (and loves) my sister and me.

When my sister and I got too old to attend our private pre-school and kindergarten, my daddy took my mother to court in the attempt to get us, by legal enforcement, into a Catholic school. He felt it was time to begin a solid education embedded in the teachings of Christ, and it was also his way of maintaining a real grip on our proper development as our father—for although custody was jointly shared, we lived primarily with our mother.

My mother abhorred the Catholic idea, and insisted that we go to public schools. Instead of working out the issue in mature discussion, there was a yearlong battle in front of a judge, which lassoed my own little five-year old self and my nine-year-old sister, into the courtroom.

What is a five-year-old supposed to say to an imposing stranger in a black robe, sitting high behind a wooden altar, when asked where she wants to go to school? With my own mother and father sitting what seemed miles away in the cold, haunted, downtown St. Louis courtroom audience, staring pointedly at their little daughter ... which one of these two was that little girl supposed to please with her "correct" answer? There is no greater sensation of being totally alone than in that very moment.

It was only the beginning of my soul's temporary waning from my spirit. Confusion, hurt, and sorrow were beginning to weigh heavily in my little heart, clouding my mind, clouding my Truth vision of the light of the HUM. And the world before my eyes was all that I began to see.

After sitting in silence in response to the judge's thrice repeated question, I finally responded, "I just want to do what my mommy and daddy want me to do. I do not know what that is."

I now know that there were Angels in the room at that very moment, doing their best to comfort me, but to no avail. My parents' emotional body of lies blocked them from my Awareness. I know this because, as I have stated before, the supernatural Miracles that God has blessed me with have enabled me to crisscross time, and I have been given insight and visions regarding certain points in this life.

The judge made the decision that my sister and I would attend public school, to be re-evaluated in one year's time. If for any reason either one of us was unhappy, we would be legally required to attend the private, Catholic school of my daddy's choice, with my father being solely responsible for the full payment of the tuition for the both of us. My mother was pleased but concerned. My daddy was unhappy, resentful, but prepared to make manifest what he desired as necessary for our highest well being.

Upon writing this, I recognize that this experience is the least of what some children must endure in court battles between unrepentant souls. Even so, it set the stage for my total distrust of either parent, of other people in positions of authority, and it deeply hurt my place of communion in the ceaseless outpouring of Christ's Love. Life, however, carried on.

As that five-year-old child, I was still a joyous soul. I was a non-stop chatterbox, curious about everything and intrigued with learning, reading, music and art. To start a brand new school with the mysterious but exciting promise of attending first grade with real individual desks and one teacher's homeroom—which would become my safe haven—was the best thing that could happen! I did not care if it was a public or a private school. I was going to school!

Throughout that whole year, my daddy tried to buy my love in preparation for his next move in court. My sister and I saw him every Wednesday night, and we were with him every other weekend at his home in south St. Louis, in accordance with the custody agreement. On those Wednesday evening outings, he laid out the red carpet, taking us out to eat and then spending the evening at one of three different St. Louis area malls. He bought us books and toys during our lazy and greedy after dinner meanderings around all those smiling mannequins in plasti-sheen department stores. I even remember that a few clerks in the toy store came to know us by name, because of our regular visits on those worldly Wednesday nights.

My sister and I would then be dropped off back at our mother and step-dad's house, overloaded with plastic bags of newly bought dolls, play sets, books, and worthless trinkets, most of which were tossed out over the years. With my mother receiving us at the door, smiling on the outside, but with heart heavy at seeing the materially bought happiness on our own faces, we would proceed to tell her of all our latest adventures with our "Daddy Warbucks", oblivious to her hurt.

My daddy was really attempting to buy our love, giving my sister and me what he never dreamed of having as a child himself. He was trying to be Healed of the experiences of lack he had endured growing up in the rural tropical islands, trying to forget about the real suffering and death he had seen, while also trying to convince us that Catholic school was the best education for us.

It was the worst thing he could have done for his own soul's health, and dangerous as well to the developing conscious minds of his only daughters.

But how could a child turn against her father's wishes, when she was treated like a little princess? I was his "Nene", his little girl, and I wanted to remain absolutely perfect in his eyes.

Come spring of first grade, I made the announcement to my mother that I wanted to go to Catholic school for second grade and never leave thereafter. My sister followed suit in her choice, and the deal was set in court.

My daddy could not have been more pleased with me for taking the initiative and, of course, that made me the apple of his eye ever more so. All seemed wonderful and lovely for a time when, from 2nd grade to 4th, I could do no wrong, as he saw it. Naturally disposed to hard and studious work, I always had straight A and often straight A+ report cards, was skilled at all the many sports I chose to participate in, and briefly took an interest in the piano classes he paid for me to take.

Those Wednesday night outings soon became an opportunity for the horrid display of his favoritism for myself over my sister. He often slipped me more money than he gave her, as we would leave his car on Report card nights. Her As and B+s were not as worthy, so it seemed, to my hurting and hurtful, but strangely loving father.

It was good that we only saw him every other weekend, because we then had a full Monday through Friday and every other weekend to forget about the random hell fires of his unpredictable ego-eruptions during the times we were with him.

What set him off was never anything of import at all. He would be in the kitchen helping one of my aunties, my *titas*, to prepare a dinner meal, and a missing utensil that he wanted at that moment would suddenly become some family member's insidious attempt to steal from him, and he acted like he really believed it to be a malicious action against him. We were all accused of stealing something from him, frequently, which of course, not a one of us ever did.

Throwing something breakable was also one of his demon-thought's favorite past-times. He was a collector of antiques and artistic glassware. He was actually a hoarder of "precious items", and it was those precious items that met their shattered fate, one by one, and over and over, subject to the whim of his acidic emotional volcanoes. My sister and I learned to run away fast, and at the drop of a hat, because we knew what was coming the moment daddy lost his temper.

There was one time when a huge conch shell was his ballistic missile, after he realized that I had not taken out the trash as he had asked of me. I really want to maintain my belief that he was not truly aiming for my head, but nevertheless, my head was in the direct line of the shell's trajectory. I was watching TV, and with laser sharp instinct, I ducked with lightning speed as the shell crashed into the wall immediately behind my head. I ran up the stairs, threw myself onto the bed, and hid my head underneath the pillow to muffle the sounds of his screaming rage. An hour later, I came downstairs to see him asleep with a book over his face. I looked behind the couch to see hundreds of finely shattered white and pink particles of the shell, embedded in the maroon shag carpet.

No one vacuumed back there for quite some time. When a house is filled with hurt, it usually stays not just under the carpet, but hidden in its deepest corners. The conch shell, which had taken many years to form in the ocean waves of the lush tropical islands of my father's homeland, would lie broken in our house until the day of my daddy's death, some 17 years later. At that time it was a strong symbol to me of my own disconnection from the HUM and from a happiness that seemed to have evaporated overnight.

Life was beginning to feel broken to that little girl.

But it was my dear Filipino stepmother who received the heaviest blow of it all, for she had to live with him, and she was the mother of his only beloved son, my half-brother. She herself had made huge sacrifices: first by leaving her own family on a small and remote Philippine island and coming to America, then by marrying my father when I was six years old, and then by giving up her own medical practice as a doctor to become a full-time, stay-at-home mother. Her biggest sacrifice beyond all comprehension was her willingness to stay in the abusive marriage she had committed to for life—and to which she remains in commitment, although now a widow. To my knowledge, he never beat her; never hit her, but the fear he instilled in her every day was, in some ways, far worse.

Even so, we all deeply loved and cherished daddy. Even though our minds and souls were being poisoned first by his energies and then by our own choice to house them and make them our own, our love for him was the Forgiveness of Christ. By way of our pure love for Daddy, we gave to him the Christ. The Holy Spirit and the collective Faith of our family brought us, somehow, through those years of hell on Earth.

Daddy's good sides were strongly loving, cheerful and funny, and with an intellect and soulful attunement to things of the supernatural that most could not comprehend. He was a charmer in all ways because he really loved learning and life, and he made his whole career a service for the souls of others in his own version of psychiatric treatment. (He nearly lost his medical license when it was discovered that he was not actively prescribing medications for his patients, but was spending the office visit time exploring their relationship to their own soul and, as each patient was inclined, with God.)

Daddy just would not do the soulful and spiritual work required by Christ to exorcise from his own precious being the layers upon layers of evil lies that he had stuffed away in his mind and body. He would not except Truth Salvation and live it for his own sake or for the sake of his Children and family. The evil energy was so thick and its expression so addictive, that he yielded to it.

Eventually, it would lead to his diagnosis of congestive heart failure in 1991, and he would die from it at the age of 60, eight years later. Oh, my beloved daddy! O, my precious *tai*!

***

Nurturing Good Amongst Evil

Oh, the never-ending spiral of Truth within the chaos and the lies! Oh, how Christ's love still radiates even with heartache that seemed it would never end! Oh, the anger of the stuffed hurt, the sorrow, the secrets, the horror! Oh, the pain of falling away from the Love of God in disbelief that there is even such a Thing!

Such is the story of many billions of people upon this planet, then and now, until He Comes Again.

This is a reminder that this entire book is the Radiance of the Holy Spirit's HUM, in washing every psyche of mankind unto the Purity of Christ's Love. It is mine to do, and I do it in each and every typed letter and page. All Praise and Glory unto our Lord Who Lives!

I truly know, beyond a shadow of a doubt, that my attendance at that private Catholic school for those five years was literally a manifested saving Grace of God's Hand. Even though the decision had been born by the order of a court of man, I know that had I not gone to Catholic school, with Mass every morning before school, Monday through Friday, my spiritual and soulful life would have permanently ended forever, with no Miracle of God's Salvation to bring it forth in resurrection. For I would not have made it in this world at all, were it not for the Holy Spirit's Fire, nourishing me with just enough reception on my part, to see me through the years.

I absolutely adored Mass, especially the Holy Eucharist. I loved the mystical energy of the combination of the sacred songs, the rhythmic regularity of the priest's words, the sharing of the Holy Gospel, and the circular Church with its Rainbow-stained glass windows. LIGHT pervaded the whole of my being, every morning at 6:30 am when Holy Mass began, and the cleansing and Healing attention of the Beloved Christ, and our Precious Virgin Mother, was felt tangibly by myself as that little child. Unlike most of my classmates, I looked forward with excitement to another school day, when yet another Mass was to be held, another Holy Eucharist was to be shared, and all my woes were temporarily unknown.

However, when the sacrament of Reconciliation came about for me, and regular confession of sins became a part of my monthly routine, my mind started to get ugly with all my unanswered questions, the guilt over my father's rage, and disgust with my own changing female body. What attunement I had to my true spirit battled with my polluted soul-mind, and I just could not shake the reverberations of my father's words, telling me when I was eight years old that my mother was a "White devil" and that, as her daughter, I had to watch out that I "did not grow horns like her."

These hateful words haunted me, and I came to abhor the knowing that my child body would soon grow into a woman's body, with no control or say on my part over what happened. I did not know what he really meant by his threat upon my future, and I certainly was pained to hear him call my mother, whom I wanted to protect and loved very much, a "devil." It both scared and outraged me. I told my mother nothing of it, and had no reply to my daddy. Instead, I took it all out on myself.

***

STRIKE THREE FOR THE HUM

By the age of nine, I had virtually shut off my ability to see the HUM or to radiate It, although I still heard and felt It at night. At such a tender age, I had no desire to assist in anybody's Healing, and it came to pass that I was no longer interested in even being in a body on Earth.

There was another family member so very dear to me who also suffered terribly in her mind because of her experience with my daddy. To protect her identity, I shall not refer to her familial relation to myself, as she is still alive, (Praise God, she overcame the horrors of her own childhood!) and I wish to respect her privacy. But seeing this family member become catatonically depressed overnight, unable or unwilling to respond to any thing or anyone at such a young age was too much for me to bear. Even when the family would go to visit her in the hospital, I chose to stay at my mother's house, alone.

And now we will observe how the world of man's glorification of disconnection through Hollywood and media intertwined with one little girl's already harrowed soul, and pulled her further down into the depths of worldly hell.

Parents, exercise STRONG caution regarding what you allow your children to be exposed to via television, the internet, movies and popular music. The number one way that the minions of evil now successfully reach the whole of a child's mind is through the lustful attraction of worldly entertainment and idolatry of professional sports. The home front should be a sanctuary, a refuge in God's Truth. It should be the place where any person can go to be recharged in God and cleansed of the world outside. My own two Children never knew what a TV was until they were about 6 years old, and we only included a TV in our home so as to watch DVDs a few years ago. We still do not watch any TV programs of any type and are not connected to a TV cable. The Children are all the stronger for this choice I made in my Mothering. Healing choices must be made in every moment. But in my Childhood, my little soul-mind felt alone, deeply confused, and hurt, so I was incapable of making such choices.

After watching a made-for-TV movie on the life of Karen Carpenter, who eventually died of a heart attack after years of anorexia, I started to restrict my eating, and began to engage in bulimic behavior as well. I loved singing and was blessed with a strong and engaging voice of my own. I thought Karen's voice to be mesmerizing, her life story romantic, and her own mental suffering was something I identified with. As pitiful as it may sound, a dead woman's soul became more of an interest to me than the comfort I gained from my beloved adoration of Mass.

No one in my family was aware of my bulimia, as that behavior was kept entirely secret, but my mother did notice that I was watching the recording of Karen Carpenter over and over, memorizing those haunting and lovely songs word for word. This was just plain wrong.

Had there been healthy adult eyes to diligently watch over and guide me I would not have been allowed to immerse myself in such world-sanctioned and popular woes. But my habit of eating very little and then disappearing into the bathroom immediately after dinner could not go unnoticed forever.

The bulimia was a plain cry for much needed attention, a slow but intentional form of suicide. A serious demonic energy had successfully entered my consciousness.

It was my loving step-dad who would be the first to figure it all out and the first to command medical intervention at that point in my life. I will always thank him for his truly loving nature and dedicated fatherhood in making me his "adopted" daughter. He stuck by my mom through the thick and thin of all those crazy years, and he has become a wonderful grandfather to my own two children.

***

A Second Dad

My step-dad had come into my life when I was six years old, and I loved him very much immediately. I thought it was great that now I could have "two dads", and I always treated him with a joyful heart. I loved talking with him about everything of interest to my questing mind. And he too considered me to be just wonderful.

He and my mother were two peas in the same pod of social justice. Even though it was a professional relationship that brought them together, their views of the world regarding issues of injustice and social and economic iniquities became their soulful bond. They were and are still committed to seeing mankind's dramas through the lens of ideologies that go far beyond the "political left." Beyond that, there is a strong love that they feel for each other, and even though they would not admit it, there is a spiritual knowing of each other that brought them together in this life.

Although born to a German-American Lutheran family, my second dad rejected his Christian upbringing, espousing socialism as his "personal religion." He was a young attorney who dedicated his career to civil rights and workers' rights issues. Together he and my mother built a law practice dedicated to helping low-income people and minorities. I viewed my parents' work with awed humility, clearly seeing that they dedicated themselves to assisting others who were so direly in need and whose circumstances were in sharp contrast to my own—those of a child attending a private school surrounded by children of wealthy families. It struck my heart in a powerful and healthy way to have this modeling of God's Golden Rule as the centering of their lives. But they always left Jesus the Christ out of it.

I grew up in two households, The split residency exposed me to opposing views and contrasting belief systems, as my biological daddy was a conservative, Roman Catholic, who voted a straight Republican ticket—always. Yet my first daddy, too, served people in need throughout a career of humility, keeping his fees for service extremely low so that most of his clients could actively afford his psychiatric practice.

So, while I was hearing about the working class, the history of Eugene Victor Debs, Che Guevara, Dr. Martin Luther King, and others like them, and being schooled in information regarding the prominent figures of the Industrial Workers of the World in the house of my mother and step-dad, I was hearing about Jesus Christ, the history of the Catholic Church in relation to warfare in unchristian lands, Outer Space, and poetry in the house of my biological daddy. All three of my parents were incredibly learned, incredibly knowledgeable in their areas of study and expertise, and all three loved to expound upon what they knew.

I became a great listener because of this odd triangle of deep intellect coming from both houses, and although my mother and step-dad never told me to stop believing in

Christ as the Savior, Redeemer, and Healer, their own words were most assuredly understood.

In their custody, I was brought to all sorts of demonstrations for social justice, pickets, rallies, and a weekly coffee house where their friends came to talk about imperialism, racism, sexism, and more. My mom and step-dad held an annual Winter Party—they had stopped calling it a "Christmas Party" very early on—where hundreds of well-known civil and social rights activists came to our house in the mostly White suburban neighborhood where we lived. Blacks, Whites, Asians, Christians, Jews, Muslims, old, and middle aged men and women piled into our house every December on the designated eve. Hundreds of people gathered to chat while enjoying the bountiful food prepared by my mother, my sister and me. (My step-dad excused himself of that activity all those years, claiming his "cultural German Lutheran" ways as justification for his non-participation in the kitchen activities in the early years, although he is now slightly more interested in cooking.)

What a wild and diverse combination of parental energies I was tossed between! I found it puzzling and ironic that my mother and step-dad had so completely rejected their Christian upbringing and Faith in God Almighty while adhering to their own version of Christ's Golden Rule, labeled as "socialism".

Remember that I attended a Catholic elementary school from 2nd to 6th grade, followed by 7th grade at a Catholic girls' school, where I found the teachings of Christ to be so clear, so simple to accept and follow. Contrast that with what I experienced in the houses of my parents. Even though my first daddy was a devout

Catholic, I often saw him turn into a demonic beast on a most unpredictable basis! In the other of my childhood houses, I heard that "religion is the opiate of the masses", and that the only way there would be equality between the races and sexes was if economic inequality was socially corrected by the people's decision to take over the American government with some strange brand of democratized socialism.

Thus is depicted the combined chaos of world and religious views, love and interest for their children, passionate professionalism, and evil energies that permeated the minds of all three of my parents. And I was always in the middle of it, barraged from all sides, all the time.

***

The Teenage Years: Soul-Battles with the World while Spirit Still Speaks

How was my own mind developing in the midst of all that? To what degree was my spirit in control of my life? I was a complex soul as a teenager, wrought with deeply stuffed negative emotions, a soul that still retained some attunement to the HUM, however waveringly, and these years were the final lap before the death that brought me to LIFE.

I continued to be a very active student, making straight As and, taking my studies quite seriously. I fully conceived of myself as becoming an astronaut—until my mother negated that idea—a medical doctor, or an international relations attorney.

My dedication and passion for learning combined with my successes in school paved the way for a bright professional future, and all my parents were greatly pleased. Even amidst the early bulimia, I still forged ahead and maintained my work as a child on Earth.

After elementary school, I spent the year of 7th grade at a prestigious Catholic girls' school, intending to follow my sister's footsteps by attending high school there. But then rebellion took hold of my worldly mind, and spurred by my desire to "experience what real kids look like," but more out of anger towards my biological daddy's years of rage, I announced that I was not returning to that "uppity" high school. I wanted to be enrolled in the local public high school.

My first daddy was crushed, but of course, my mother and step-dad were overjoyed.

I continued to ace all of my classes, quickly moving into the honors program in 8th grade, and staying in all of the honors and AP courses throughout high school. I earned college credit because of all the advanced classes I took, and I always landed the main role in many high school thespian productions over those four years. Everything looked great on the outside, for the most part. But the volcano was heating up on the inside. I became even more rebellious in my thinking about the world, choosing to see more along the lines of my mother and step-dad rather than my first dad.

The history of oppression against minorities was a favorite topic that I began to delve into. I came to be a mini-expert regarding the Lakota, Hopi, Cherokee and Dine history of Native Americans in the USA. Little did I know at the time that while my conscious reasoning looked for proof of what the "White man" had always done to people of color, my real interest in this had more to do with my spirit still speaking through my mind, over and above the voice of my ego. This is a clear example of how the Holy Spirit still managed to weave through that chaotic teenage mind, commanding me to focus upon SOMETHING of spiritual worth, if not on Christ Himself.

At 13-15 years old, I held a strong but secretive conviction that I was very close to the Ancestors, and I developed a definite belief in Wakan Tanka, or the Great

Spirit. This was not the Christian God of Whom I had been taught in Catholic school, but my notion of Creator as guided by Native American spirituality, and which became the means by which God Almighty maintained a grip on my soul.

What I know now is that God does not care how one labels Him in names or titles, using human words, as these are thinner than mica and without spiritual substance. What God cares about is a heart, mind and soul GIVEN to Him in FULL. This is the essence for the genesis of Forgiveness.

Jesus was still taking command over my mind, to the degree that I was able to Receive His Energy, by way of my true Faith in the Great Spirit's mysterious and sacred bounty of the stars, Nature, and the Earth. These Ancestors to whom I so often spoke quietly were indeed a spiritual lifeline for my chaotic outer life. When in Nature, I revered them in awe, and before eating meals I began the ritual of reserving a portion of my food in a napkin to then offer to the Earth when finished, and in Prayer of Gratitude. No one on Earth taught me to do that, as it was born of my spiritual belonging to those on the Other Side.

It would be 15 years later, when my spirit had successfully come to dominate the whole of my consciousness, that I would be given memories of just how I am, indeed, truly linked to some Lakota Grandmothers and Grandfathers. This mystical and supernatural Awareness is not at all contrary to my belonging to Jesus the Christ, but is a gift of attunement given to me in part because of the huge path of Healing from God by which I have now been cleansed. The more devotion one brings to one's walk in communion with ELOI, the more the imprints and limitations of mankind's thinking simply evaporate, and the boundless TRUTH reigns triumphant in the mind, body, and heart. Truth is divinely supernatural, and no man or religion can claim It as its own.

***

THE FIRE OF INFINITY BREATHES

One of the most important teachings I wish to radiate from this book is that yes, Jesus Christ IS the Way, the Truth, and the Life. But He was only sent as a form of God Almighty, as the Son of God, because mankind had so evilly espoused the ways of the devil and no longer has the ability to see TRUTH. TRUTH is eternal, and It had been everywhere on Earth before man's chosen fall. As a Ray of God's Body, Truth is an inherent part of ALL life, and all pure Life is divinely supernatural.

What I am getting at is this: JESUS has been co-opted by worldly Christianity as if He belongs only to the churches and religiosity of this world. I tell you clearly that He is Above and beyond any and all churches, any and all religions, and most obviously Above and beyond man and mankind's world. Knowing you belong to Jesus the Christ in FULL IS the embodiment of His Church.

There ARE certain groups of people who, in certain spaces of time on Earth, were given the wisdom of ELOI to embody as a people, among them, some groups of Native Americans. To Worship Creator as revealed through the mysteries of Nature, these Ancestors were able to tune into themselves as spirit beings of the stars, temporarily on Earth, as they lived and breathed constant, loving Adoration of God. Some of them were given the awareness that in the future, there would be just One Man, born in a land far from where they were, who would indeed be God in human form.

But all fall short of the glory of God. There is not one single civilization, no nation or people who has had any chosen consistency in embodying TRUTH, and in living the Will of God alone, upon this world. That is why, throughout the history of mankind, peoples and civilizations have been wiped away in the blink of an eye. God's Great Plan on Earth requires a proper balance, and when evil becomes the norm, the inevitable cleansing has always come to pass.

Now, with evil having been embraced as the collective reality for mankind in all of its myriad demonic faces, humanity STILL has not repented of its chosen abominations, STILL has not come to accept the cosmic TRUTH of God's Majesty and God's Will, and STILL is battling itself with endless manifestations of disconnection and dis-ease. God foresaw that JESUS is the Way for mankind to make God's Presence known again, but as is clearly obvious, the majority of Earth residents consider themselves to be mere humans and they collectively hate the ONE sent, Who Saved those who are chosen. Therefore, many have been called over millions of years, but those who are chosen by the ONE God are few indeed.

This is not religious fanaticism, this is not religious supremacy—this is TRUTH. If you want to have a Rejuvenated Life in God's Love and Might, and more importantly, if you want to continue on in the TRUTH of God's endless Body of Infinity, then you better crush your addictions to ego and to the world and throw yourself into God's Miraculous Light.

Mankind may be blind and dying, but I am one who Breathes what I SEE, for all who would choose to Receive Him.

***

A Woman of God's Love and Two Women of the Qualities of the Divine Mother

My own biological mother, who is not my eternal mother, was chosen by THE ONE GOD to bring forth my human form, but she does not understand this nor would she presently accept the supernatural Truth of it. She will not accept that she is a soul in this world, with an individual spirit, and that God chose her to be the one who would bring my body into this last lifetime on Earth. She cringed, when at four years of age I told her, "You are not my REAL Mother," as many women on Earth probably would. Even though she still refuses to accept and live the TRUTH that God IS the Savior Jesus Christ and more, I will always love and Pray for her soul, that she may choose to Return to His Infinite Power well before she leaves her own physical body.

In the beginning, my Earth mother did embody many of the sacred energies of God's Plan for her as my mother. When she met my father, she still had Faith in God, but that changed over time, and I have already highlighted the reasons why her mind chose to stray from such an awesome and Perfect Relationship.

In this short section, I give respectful attention to that part of her soul that was strong in this way, and I write in my ongoing Prayerful focus that she will yet choose to fully Return to Christ, well before she leaves her body, as it is still alive on Earth. The cold hard Truth reveals that if one is attempting to eek out a life without Christ, one is a walking dead soul. I do not envision a permanent end for the spirits of either my mother or my step-dad. I want both of them to be given permission to Return to the starry places from which they came, but of which they have no memory because of their chosen disconnections in this worldly lifetime. May they CHOOSE to accept the Truth of Who God IS, in repentance, and may God shower Mercy upon the whole of their being.

I will now highlight two angelic women who helped raise me, neither blood-related, but very much my spirit aunties in God's Eternity. My biological daddy had a brother whose Filipina wife was truly an embodiment of the Divine Mother for my sister and me. She came to America after marrying my uncle, and from the very beginning of my own life, she was there raising me as if I was her own child. She, my uncle, their son (my cousin), and another sister of my father's all lived with us in the duplex that my father owned.

She was born in the Philippines on June 27, 1936, three years before my own first daddy, and he playfully joked with her as if she was his own grandma because of her few short years as his senior. She really was the quiet Queen Bee of the household before my biological mother, or my daddy's second wife, came into our lives.

My *tita* was always the one to do most of the cooking, most of the cleaning, and all of the bathing of the three of us Children on the weekends when my sister and I were in my daddy's custody. She is the one who taught me how to say the Rosary before bed at night. She is the one who hummed happy devotional songs to Christ as she prepared *pancit, puto,* and chicken *adobo* in the family kitchen. She is the one whose tender voice and gentle smile always comforted me when she tucked my sister and me into bed, and she was the one who secretly found her way to us soon after my daddy had one of his emotional explosions, for I so needed a cornerstone of the Blessed Virgin Mary upon whose lap I could escape and seek refuge.

When my own mother became so busy with her new lawyer lifestyle soon after I was born, always needing a babysitter when we were in her custody, she came to my *tita* for help. We were dropped off to stay with her early in the morning, to be picked up by my mother in the late afternoon. So in all truth, I know I spent more hours and days of those precious early formative years with my beloved *tita*, than I did with my own mother. This is not a judgment of my mother, as she was working amazingly hard to become a professional woman in a difficult world, as well as having to deal with my daddy even though divorced. It is simply the sharing of fact. I love them both so deeply.

I have never known any other being in this world that has prayed the Rosary every single night for over 50 years, the way my *tita* has. She has remained steadfast in her ever-growing Faith for all of her nearly 80 years. Regardless of the sufferings known and unknown that she witnessed in the Philippines and in her personal life, she has always truly embodied the Grace, poised Nurturance, and Unconditional Love of the Blessed Virgin Mary, as well as the Christ. *Praise God!*

My *tita* bore all the suffering of a lost baby daughter of her own (born before my male cousin) and I believe that this was part of the reason that she was overjoyed to mother both my sister and me. She still talks of that sweet soul who left her body so early, and in the same breath reminisces about me as a baby and toddler. Her nurturing cooking, her amazing piano playing, and her Faithful home-maker soul was the very anchor of my being unto the Love of God, and without her as the embodiment of the Divine Mother's nurturing care and providence, I truly do not think I could have come to the place I am now.

My other *tita*, who was actually the second wife of my first daddy, is also the embodiment of True Gentleness, demure calm, and intelligence. She became a medical doctor in the Philippines before she came to America and married my daddy. She was a pediatrician whose heart truly loved all children and Life itself. The sacrifice she made in staying married to my daddy, who made so much of her daily life a fearful existence, (although he never physically abused her) bearing and raising a son and giving up her medical practice to be a good mother and wife, is phenomenal to me.

When my biological daddy was first diagnosed with congestive heart failure, his whole demeanor changed. No longer was the rage present. He had made the decision to travel to Yugoslavia to visit the holy site of Medjugorie, where the Virgin Mary had repeatedly appeared to the young Children. He felt confident that he would be fully Healed of his condition. My *tita* and my brother went with him, and over a space of time, both before and after this major trip, my daddy became a changed man.

It was a Miracle in itself that my daddy, in such a short space of time, became a totally Renewed soul. I know now that the experience of being diagnosed with such a fatal condition, combined with his devout Faith in the WORD was the exact combination that made him choose to submit to the Holy Spirit for the REAL Healing of his heart and soul. His eternal spirit was finally able to take some hold on his Earthly life. And his beloved wife, my *tita*, was the soul who God had sent so that her own amazing Faith and Unconditional Love would see him through until he died, and beyond.

With the diagnosis of heart failure, my daddy knew he would soon retire from his own medical work. At that time, my *tita* decided to study all over again to resume her career as the doctor she was before she married. According to law, she needed to renew her medical license, and in order to do that she needed to take the latest exams. In spite of the increasing financial stress of the medical bills and the knowledge that her husband's life was beginning to end, and while raising my younger brother, she spent night after night studying hard, updating herself on the complications of the medical texts of the early 90s. After high hopes and much preparedness, she missed passing the grueling test by one point. She decided God was showing her that it was not a part of His Will for her to become a medical doctor again, so she went to nursing school instead.

My *tita* is an intelligent, gracious, and devout woman; a medical doctor who humbly chose to become a nurse because she has always chosen to submit to the workings of the Holy Spirit, and to focus on the well-being of her family. I have never seen this beloved and dear *tita* of mine ever say or do anything that was in the slightest self-centered or selfish.

All three of these mothers were and are amazing to me for their sacrifices, for their brilliance, for their humility, and for their unique emanations of Christ's Love. Part of my motherhood and of my soul's own radiance is credited to what I saw in these women. I will always hold onto the rays of Joy with which they nourished me over our time together.

Praise God!

***

THE CONCLUSION OF ELISE'S FAMILY ALBUM

This concludes the brief description of those primary ones in my Earthly life who are so unutterably dear to me in the Indomitable Love of Christ. My whole being cherishes each and every one of them, and this Ray becomes ever stronger as I reflect on them as I write this book.

In the polarity of my Childhood family homes—from leftist social activists who nurtured my intellect and worldly mind, to the devout Christians who came from the other side of the world to raise me in the Holy Spirit—I grew into adulthood. Because God put me in an ethnically rich family that honored all peoples of this world as worthy of loving respect and Goodness, and because each of them, in their own unique way, embodied some frequency of the Christ, my spirit has so merged with my own beautiful soul in Perfection.

There are a few more important members of my extended spiritual family who had a powerful place in my life. In my own quiet way, I continue to Pray for them all, and I ask their forgiveness for not directly including them in this book. (If I did, it would be thousands of pages long!) You know who you are to me and, more importantly, God sees who you are and what you have done in His Life. I thank you so deeply, and am so happy that I know you for eternity! Bless God!

And now, I throw myself into the ocean of God's Infinity with ever more Rejoicing! Please, return with me now to your own focused inhale, for I want you to understand the magnitude of all you have just read.

You have just communed with a new Ray of God's Healing for yourself, your immediate family, and for all life on Earth. The Healing of Christ has fired through the whole of your being, through every single atom and every wave of your thought by way of reading this book. I know this because of what I have lived through, what I have been Graced with by God, and what I have Returned to as the very essence of my supernatural being. God's Life and Body is Divinely supernatural, and your heart is a part of this awesome Gift. I want you to KNOW this and to live it fully in Worship of God Almighty! I want you to embody Infinity now.

***

Weaving God's Timeless Healing While Living In Earth Time

We now examine the details of the latter part of my life on Earth. Again, I will weave in and out of linear time to tell you about the early days of my Healing ministry while reflecting back to the manifestations of dis-ease and cleansing I subjected myself to. Death at age 20 was just the first. More destruction and disconnection was to come.

My purpose in writing in this way is because I must, in accordance with the Guidance of the Holy Spirit to Whom my whole being belongs. I am in human form and was locked into this third dimensional reality by way of the sufferings and trauma of the mind. As I have pointed out, however, my spirit never truly left this body temple, even in the darkest recesses of my soul. God would not allow it by His Divine Grace and Mercy. He knew what my spirit has always been devoted to—assistance to mankind—and He knew what I would choose to Return to in time.

However, I am an eternal spirit being who now lives within and beyond time, and even though this body I use is indeed fully alive within this dying world, my abilities to see through everything about it must be expressed in such a non-linear fashion. In doing so, I am assisting you in re-focusing your own vision of the stories of your life. What you develop your soul into, what you experience in this lifetime, is all intended for the cleansing of God's Body in this part of the Milky Way Galaxy. To have just one more soul come to the full realization that it is a unique spirit in communion with and belonging to God Alone, will make manifest the Healing of God's Creation Frequency for all who remain in grave need. God's Will is thus.

In the following portion of this book, I will speak of the testimonial and music ministry I was called to begin 13 years ago: Voice of Christ's Healing. But in order to depict for you how it was born and the core Fire of its Purpose, I also need to share the rest of the impossible Miracles manifested through my life. A successful suicide and resurrection at age 20 was not the least of God's Miraculous Hand at work.

Right now, I am feeling my muscle fibers separating in an ecstatic release, but I am doing nothing more than sitting in front of a computer and typing. It is as if my upper torso is being squeezed by a giant's Hand. It is intense, but wonderful, and as I breathe with another delicious inhale, I feel the HUM cascading as my flesh. Another sacred example of how His Holy Rays are nonstop in outpouring.

I cannot logically explain how my muscles developed scar tissue around all these healed bones. X-rays taken when I was 30 found that the previous diagnosis of severe osteoarthritis resulting from childhood injury and anorexia was no longer relevant.

But as I take my intentionally accentuated inhales, my head lifts up from the stacks of my vertebrae, making more space in between the discs, and I feel the pulling tightness of fibrous protein threads, fused together in knot-like fashion. I feel them being burned of their accumulated tension. Years and years of lies, still being stripped and streamed away from this beautiful body temple of Christ.

> *Oh, sweet Lord, there is always more to release unto You, isn't there? And You, my Holy King, are ALWAYS here, to take it from us all. How I love You, my ELOI! My love can never be as strong and perfect as Yours, but I keep going deeper in my determination to be breathed through fully, in Your Perfection.*

In and out of brief moments of time on Earth, in and out of human evils, in and out of this false-face world, in and out of mental and bodily restrictions and entrenched worldly belief systems, in and out of the ocean of God's Loving Truth. Why does mankind make God's Life so hard for itself? Why is mankind destroying itself?

I remind you that the devil is already defeated.

My command to this world is: STOP EMBODYING THE WAYS OF THE DEVIL. SUBMIT AND YIELD TO THE INDOMITABLE LOVE OF GOD'S WILL.

And be honest about what you cannot do, and what God will do the very moment you fully submit and yield to His Awesome Truth and Love.

***

On Becoming a Messenger of Infinity

I have spent hours in a question-and-answer period following one of my ministerial presentations, making sure that all questions and respectful comments are addressed and answered to the best of my ability, for you should be TRANSPARENT in Truth if and when the Holy Spirit guides you to speak of a Miracle through your life, either one-on-one, or to a group. If one gives enough proper space, listening exclusively to the Will of God in all circumstances, one will truly be the master of what one has experienced, so as to perfectly reach others in Truth.

God Almighty had to prepare me for four and a half years before He could see that I was ready to speak before large audiences. At first I was willful, egotistically driven about taking "my show on the road." In the first year after my heart attack, when I was fully, physically recovered, and I was finally happy to be alive, I wanted to shout out to the world of the possibilities of overcoming depression or anything that was a physical or mental dis-ease. I organized, of my own thought and muscle, a monthly presentation on various topics of Healing, where I sought different presenters to come speak to a group who would gather in a community room of the local city library.

There was heart and soul in what I did, but no full presence of the Holy Spirit, because I was doing it of a spiritually-ego driven mindset. For "I" had so much to share because "I" had been through so much and survived, and here's what "I" could tell the world about what works in order to change your life and be healed of whatever you currently suffer from.

Huh-uh. It did not last very long. After 10 months of regular presentations, with myself finding and contacting all the presenters, printing all the fliers, posting all of those hundreds of pieces of paper on city kiosks, exclusively paying for the newspaper ads, as well as preparing and providing free organic food at each presentation, I was drained and exhausted, even though there were regular turn-outs of anywhere from 25 to 50 people. I dropped the whole endeavor after the 10th gathering of what I had named "Nourishing Vibrations."

You cannot do ANYTHING on your own and see it last, no matter how sweet it looks on the outside, for there is no foundation in Jesus Christ if you really think you are doing something of your own will. Whatever it is you are trying to bring forth may be sustained by the world for a little chunk of time and space, but it will always fall apart if it is not born of the cornerstone of God's Will.

So, after I realized that I was still acting and thinking from a dominant ego focus, I took the rest of that four years of preparation in God's Will very seriously, in contemplative Prayer, Scriptural study, and Yogic meditation.

I realized the error of my thinking, and decided to be crushed in the humble and cleansing Waters that my ego addictions needed to be drowned in, so that my own spirit could inundate me in an endless drink of His Ocean. Then the Pure Work of the Holy Spirit began. Or rather, I began to tune into the Purity of His Work and it began to flow through me with an Eagle Eye precision.

Before I begin the descriptive stream of what the Healing ministry turned into, I need to backtrack in time so as to give you a chronological summary of the events in my life. You must have a clear picture, restated, of the Miraculous space of time in which I was Healed. As I explained before, I am interweaving the whole of my life's stories, sometimes commenting on an early Childhood experience so as to give you understanding of a consequence later in life. I will not go into the details of some of the events of my life listed below, but shall summarize them here as reference for the understanding of the flow of my worldly life up to the glorious moment of Infinity in which I reside NOW. You will see how, and from what life trials, this Healing ministry was born.

January 5, 1977: I was born in a blizzard in St. Louis, Missouri, USA, to a Filipino father and Caucasian American mother. A few months later I was baptized in the Catholic Church.

Advent season 1982: I suffer broken vertebrae and cranial fractures after a gymnastics accident. God Heals and restores my little body in the Prayerful circle of Filipino family and friends. X-rays and MRI show no fracture, but signs that there had been trauma to the bones.

1984: I begin to attend Catholic school. In our parish church, I receive the Sacraments of Reconciliation and the Holy Eucharist at age 7.

1986: I receive the Sacrament of Confirmation at age 9. I show myself to be a studious, bright, straight-A student who loves reading, music, art, writing, learning, and school.

Spring 1990: I was admitted to a psychiatric in-patient program for bulimia and suicide prevention watch, at the age of 13.

Good Friday 1997: At age 20, my flesh was declared medically dead by suicide. I was Saved and restored into my body, 3 hours later by God Almighty.

August 1998: I returned to Columbia, Missouri, for the continuation of my University studies, which I had left as a freshman in Spring 1996, due to increased suicidal tendencies. My father, Dr. Pacelli Brion, was well on his way towards death due to congestive heart failure.

Spring 1999: My boyfriend proposes to me and I accept. A ceremony is planned for May of 2000.

August 24, 1999: Dr. Pacelli Escondo Brion dies. I am living in a city 120 miles away from him, with my boyfriend. I am increasingly anorexic and exercising excessively. The deterioration of my skeletal system, diagnosed as osteoarthritic four year previous, accelerates as my body scavenges for calcium. Loss of fat in my Eustachian tubes causes hearing loss in both ears, and I show signs of heart failure.

December 1999: At my family's insistence I see a Student Health doctor on campus. He tells me bluntly that I am anorexic and will die if I go untreated.

July 2000: I collapse with a heart attack while running on the MKT trail, in 100+ degree weather. A mysterious Angel in the form of a man who calls himself "Michael," discovers my body and carries me back to Student Health on campus, running 2 miles. No details of the man are gathered, nor is the man seen again. I weigh 95 pounds at 5'9". The same doctor who saw me in December of 1999 tells me that my parents can have no say about admitting me into an eating disorder program at Baptist Medical Center in Kansas City, Missouri as I am now of legal adult age. He leaves the contact information on a piece of paper by my bedside, and I am left to decide if I will go.

***

Anorexia or Soulful, Spiritual Cleansing?

Who is to say if that period of what I call my "second death" from a heart attack brought on by anorexia was not soulfully and spiritually necessary? I know that God's Hand and Might has always been at work in my life, even in the deepest pits of my self-created hell.

He is ALWAYS there, and never ever leaves the person who is chosen by Him. For God is the only ONE, in three Persons, Whom one can undoubtingly Trust in all circumstances on Earth. No person in this world is trustworthy and 100% reliable, but GOD IS. No other person LOVES the Way God LOVES, case closed. It is not a question of IF God will show up, but WHEN you will choose to Receive Him. All answers to life problems lie in how attentive one is in listening to and Receiving His direct Guidance.

With 22 years of lies, filth, and suffering stuffed so deeply into my conscious and sub-conscious mind, and with the toxicity of that collective sin lodged into the very marrow of my physical bones, it is clear, from an odd point of view, why I needed to go through that period of intense exorcism via a self-induced fasting. My mind had been trained to think in extremes, so an extreme measure was taken as the last straw to force me into a permanent spiritual Awakening. As crazy as it sounds to read this now, I am grateful for this period of emaciation and anorexia. I know what kind of energetic hell had accumulated in the depths of my mind and flesh up to that time. Looking back from this side of Healing I can see that there was no other way for me to have been exorcised of all that filth. I myself had created this soul-mind who thought, behaved, and reacted so dangerously. I emphatically DO NOT advocate the use of starvation or other self-destructive behaviors as a means of cleansing in Christ. I DO promote, teach, and radiate His Way of Truth, which, for humanity, is the process of undoing the lies while choosing to constantly Receive His Divinely supernatural Love.

After three months of in-patient physical rehabilitation at the hospital where I was admitted after the heart attack, and at a meager 104.5 pounds, I was faced with the decision of whether or not to admit myself to the treatment program for eating disorders in another city 200 miles away. Having nothing to do but mostly lie in a hospital bed will make a person go absolutely stir-crazy or will create a garden for soulful and spiritual awakening.

Perhaps there is some type of in-between experience or mental doldrums where one has the option to just dumb down by watching the TV all day or reading People magazine, but that was most definitely not what I chose. In this time was the beginning of my introduction to meditative Breathing as Prayer, which led to more ecstatic spiritual visions and blessed visitations from the Other Side.

In those three months of bed rest, drinking nothing but chocolate Ensure, and playing lots of rounds of Gin Rummy with a very kind and lovely nurse (who will hold a secure place in heaven for her selfless nature I Pray), I began to have memory flashes of what I had seen a while back on Good Friday of 1997. The spirits of my three future Children were calling to me, whispering to me in their perfected beauty during my glucose-heavy sleeps as I lay enshrouded in starchy White linen blankets with beeping machines all around.

I saw visions of each of them, at first just when I was sleeping, but then they came during my waking hours when I was alone in that cubed room where God's physical salvation was at work. The perfect Silver/Blue eyes of my boy, a son, first appeared to me as an infant with such Golden blonde hair. Then, in a warp of time, boundless and mystifying, I saw him around the age of six, and then again as a young man. He was stunningly beautiful and STRONG. My heart yearned for him.

I saw the image of my second Child, my first daughter as a baby, with an olive complexion like myself, and more Filipina features: a button nose and pea-shaped nostrils. She had rounded happy little cheeks and the deepest Brown eyes that shot rays of her timeless love for me through my every cell. She was Joy embodied. Through the warp of time I saw images of her scaling Trees and playing with a host of the different animals she loved. The last image of her was when she appeared to be a young teenager, sitting next to her older brother and another very young girl, their sister. I wanted this girl Child so badly. And I wanted her little sister with a Force of Passion such as I had never felt before.

I marveled at these visions, never doubting their veracity, as it was the second time I was given the Grace of these supernatural visitations of spirit beings who had not yet come into bodies. Their promise of being my Children was perfect in my awareness. Their power reached me in pure force, sparking my mind with the energies of my essence as a timeless Mother. There was something timelessly perfect about these three sacred spirit being Children. Little did I know at the time just how spiritually powerful they are, individually and as a triad. The inviolable knowing of my path of motherhood, combined with the memory that I was to become a Mother for an even greater purpose, was the very reason behind my agreement to admit myself to the eating disorder program in Kansas City.

I had not had a menstrual period in over one and a half years. I was committed to doing whatever it took to Heal and to become Whole so that I could and would become the Mother I have always been, beyond this world. All Praise and Glory to God Almighty!

I was admitted into the rehab hospital in July of 2000, and my boyfriend suggested that we postpone the date of our wedding ceremony until May 26, 2001. I was grateful for that space of time to just be replenished and work through all the mental filth. Had I fully been united with Christ at that time, and if there had been individuals around me who truly emanated the Lord, I would have rejected the endless process of strict psychological and cognitive therapy and done nothing but repent. In true acknowledgement of my long time disconnection from sweet Jesus, and in the act of giving myself up to His ceaseless streaming Love (which is part of Forgiveness), I would have immediately Retrained my brain in the Scriptural WORD that tells me He had already forgiven and cleansed me. I know, in retrospect, that had this been the choice that was modeled to me by adults in my childhood, and had this been the choice that I made before the age of 20, my life story would not have been filled with the suffering I induced. But that would have altered the course of the ministry of God's Healing through my life, if it had been created at all!

There are no regrets, no turning back, no "could-a would-a should-a". That kind of attitude is just about the most worthless little demon one can harbor in the conscious mind, as it keeps the thinker stuck in the past and lodged into the grip of addictions to negative emotional existence, providing the perfect fuel and fodder for the minions of evil to remain in the personal life and in this world.

Are you beginning to see the reality of how insidiously evil and successful a defeated devil has become through the minds of mankind? Do you feel the depravity of this and the dire results?

The very fact that human beings really believe that negative emotions are just a part of human nature is the biggest stab to the Heart of Jesus Christ. Collective humanity shows Jesus, moment by moment, day by day, that it believes His timeless and selfless Act of Atonement —His torture and crucifixion, His Blood spilling, His descent into Hell to annihilate the bonds of sin that tie mankind—is worthless and nothing. The fact that evil— manifested as rape and torture, individual, social, national, and international violence to other humans and more horrid still, to Nature and Animals—exists in this day, 2,000 years after He brought and modeled the Way to Infinity and Freedom, is an abomination to God Almighty. Collective humanity is not deserving of God's Life because it has collectively chosen to reject the Truth.

I Pray that you understand CLEARLY what I am about to say here, and receive it with an open heart. Your own mental and soulful disconnections, the sufferings you choose to hold on to, are contributing to this evil presence on sacred planet Earth. I am not saying that YOU are evil (quite to the contrary), but I am simply highlighting the truth, which is that your inability to sever your own mind from the past and from negative circumstances is a CHOICE that you have made. When this individual choice to keep your being latched onto the past, to be endlessly burdened with negative emotional weights is multiplied by billions of people ... *Lord have MERCY!* Are you beginning to understand how humanity, individual by individual, is destroying the tender network of God's Light, the Creation Frequency, which holds all life on Earth together?

You see, all matter on Earth is nothing more than concentrated filaments of cosmic light. Your body has been reduced to a biotic carbon compound of materiality and the world strives to make you believe that the scope of your existence is limited to that body. Your sacred flesh in its perfection of structure with organs and bones is composed of trillions upon trillions of micro-fibrous streams and particle waves of light that you cannot see with the naked eye. This is because your True Vision has become blinded over the millions of years that mankind has chosen to disconnect from God, choosing instead to exist according to the ways of evil. Do you see how mankind has severed itself from the cosmic nature and the Reality of belonging to God's Light?

Christianity as understood in this world has no knowledge of the fact that humanity was originally brought forth by God to Earth in energetic light form, not as the flesh. Beyond this third dimension—proven to be one of the lowest frequency realms within God's "outer space," meaning that wavelengths of light move very slowly where Earth is located in the Milky Way Galaxy—there is no carbon-based physiology in Nature. This manifestation is only here on Earth. EVERYTHING is composed of some degree of cosmic light, patterned forth by the Mind of God, but mankind is so disconnected that it no longer has the privilege to see in this way.

I am fully prepared to endure the backlash for my sharing of this fact, as my communion in Jesus the Christ protects and emboldens me in confidence and conviction. I hold no secrets and I radiate what the Holy Spirit would have me do. For all those who would question me in testing of the spirits: Yes, of course I know Jesus to be the Son of God, the ONLY Savior, Redeemer, and Healer. He is the Absolute Way, the Truth, and the Life, and yes, I am fully in communion with the Reality that He shed His Blood for the redemption and Salvation of mankind.

Why in the world would I be sharing my intensely personal life story but for the sole purpose of radiating His Will for you to be fully Healed and alive as His Infinite child? It is what I am placed upon this planet to do, and I do it with supreme focus and concentration.

The Second Person, Jesus the Christ, along with the Holy Spirit via the ONE GOD ALMIGHTY is more Divinely Supernatural than mankind will ever get a glimpse of through the conscious mind. One cannot even taste of Jesus with the conscious mind. Sure, you can read the Holy Bible and say everything that your priest or pastor tells you to say, but you need to go deeper in Returning to a personal relationship with our Holy Savior in order to even get a taste of His Majesty which has nothing to do with any person. The conscious level of the waking, thinking mind is where the religiosity of Christians on Earth limits itself. Jesus the Christ did not come through mankind to spread religion as human beings have created of it. He came to call many, but to remind those who are chosen to Return, and to remind them of their place in the Infinity of God Almighty's Kingdom.

I tell you again, receiving God's Miracles and having them consume you is a divinely supernatural gift, and one's worldly mind is no longer capable of being the lens through which Life is seen. God's Work is too big for that, and He looks for His Children who might be capable and strong enough to transmit what HE wills to be known within this world for the Good of All. Faith, which is belief in the things unseen combined with the muscle of the Holy Spirit working through one who is Graced with Faith, is a frequency that leads to understanding and then to KNOWING that the Majesty of God is, indeed, Divinely Supernatural.

But let us return now to what happened in the Rebirthing and Renewal of my being in the year 2000.

I was 23 years old, and remained as an inpatient at Kansas City Baptist Medical Center's eating disorder unit from July until September 21, when I was discharged at a weight of 118.5. I was still very thin, but I was considered to be at the lowest rung of a healthy weight for my height. Most importantly, my heart was functioning at normal capacity, which is another amazing Miracle considering the emaciation I had brought to the whole of my beautiful temple. The day after I was discharged, I attended the wedding of some college friends. I felt a hopeful Breath of renewal and excitement within my choice to immerse in Joyful living, for I was to become a MOTHER, and I knew it would be sooner than I had thought. Yet, I took a look at what I had done to my body and wondered in Prayer to God, "HOW?"

I had had no menstrual period for nearly two years, from 1998 to 2000 because of the anorexia. My reproductive system had shut down from lack of proper nourishment. My bones were severely calcium-depleted, and I had lost a great deal of cartilage between my joints, and I was diagnosed with osteoarthritis condition in my upper spine, shoulders, and neck, which I could most definitely feel.

Motherhood would have to be another Miracle made manifest. And to God we Give ALL the Praise and Glory; for another Miracle flowed forth. Here is where my story gets better, rising higher and HIGHER in our Lord Jesus Christ! Here is where the part of the ministry which is MOTHERHOOD, begins!

I was discharged from the hospital in September 2000. At the end of December of 2000, my precious menstrual flow, a sacred Gift of Life from God Almighty, returned, and I became pregnant with my first Child in February 2001.

For nearly two years I was without my period, and just two months after its return, my womb was blessed with a precious spirit being's life made manifest. The first of these Children (whose images I had seen four years prior to this first pregnancy, when my body was dead by suicide) was about to take form, blessing my Awakening in the Truth of our Lord Jesus Christ.

***

January 5, 2015:
A Journal Entry

I write my sacred little Testimony, on the night of my 38th birthday. The moon was full at midnight this morning, just as it was on the day of my birth. I used to believe that the whole of me was primarily influenced by the fact that the lunar body peaked in its fullness on that first blizzard birthday of mine. I really thought that my former outgoing, ever-social character was primarily due to the fact that I emerged unto this world exactly at the peak of a full moon. I used to believe a lot of nonsense such as this.

Little did I know in those disjointed spaces of my life, that in Truth, I am formed of, and because of He Who is beyond and greater than all universes.

Oh, how grateful I am to have rid myself of the greatest weights of ignorance, disconnection, and lies. To be constantly renewed and nourished in the ceaseless Love of Jesus Christ is to live Heaven on Earth. What an ecstatic, timeless, and boundless TREASURE to have Returned to the Truth of being nothing without God Almighty and everything within Him! Infinity is so very sweet!

Tonight I marvel because of the endless streams of God's Graces upon this little lifetime. I marvel to be *sitting here finally, sharing with you my soul and my spirit's precious gemstones of Awakening. And I marvel that God has finally seen me ready to gift this Witnessing, this revelatory work, (as small as it is) in His Scope of the Great Plan. I have waited to be here, in this very moment, for what seems to be ages, but in reality is no time at all. Let His Radiance continue to burn brighter throughout this dimension by way of these pages, so that your own amazing and accelerated Healing adds to the wondrousness of God's ceaseless Light.*

On this, my birthday evening, I quietly sang in Prayer to both of my Children as they fell asleep in their beds. It is an everyday occurrence in our home, but tonight was interfused with an especially unique stream. What came through on this night was a breath of Heaven unto this Earth, and I now translate it through the sharing of this next wave of my life story.

Not one, but TWO Children have I in the flesh, and even though I know they belong fully to our Lord Jesus Christ, I know that they are MY Children ... not just for this lifetime on Earth, but unto Eternity.

My first-born child was conceived in February of 2001, and he was born at home in the Water, a few weeks before Thanksgiving that same year. In those nine months of sacred pregnancy, I became stronger in God's Health through a commitment to the mystery of Wholeness, receiving constant streams of realizations and joy in the long Healing process that has no end while down here in form. I knew clearly that I had never before known True Health, and I was focused in my own will and determination to run the course of all that the journey entailed. To know that I was pregnant was the sealing of my covenant with God to never ever look back. Recalling that my very name, "Elise" means "an oath or covenant with God", I finally returned to a firm foundation with my eye upon the future, in the Faith He gave me.

God is supernaturally Faithful, and this awesome and supernatural energy of our Beloved Lord has no limits in its Gifting. I was receiving loads of it, for in those first few weeks of pregnancy, I became fired with the possibilities that I could see and feel regarding Healing, not just for myself, but for all who would truly LOVE God. I began to sense that my focus on His Will of Healing for my life, was a microcosm for all humanity, and there was no need to exert mental strain in empty worded prayer for others. I knew that all Life was unified, but now it was something I could feel and sink my teeth into. I was slowly beginning to feel Faith as a part of my body, as part of the very substance of my baby; it was and is a tangible frequency that when focused upon by anyone, becomes the muscle of the Holy Spirit in manifested activity. And when a person moves in action according to Faith in God's WORD, more Faith is streamed into the whole of that person's being, and His Will is done with ever more radiance.

***

ON CONFIDENCE AND HOPE

All the lies I had integrated as beliefs slowly began to melt away, and I knew that at some point in my future, my legally blind eyesight would be fully healed. I also became committed to seeing full lifting of the osteoarthritis I had been diagnosed with six years earlier. I didn't wonder or worry about how long it would take because I was absolutely confident that it would occur. There is nothing more elating than this kind of hope, this kind of joy. Truly, in every moment of every day of carrying my firstborn child, I returned to the ecstasy of Christ's nurturing Love.

As the spirit being son of mine was translated into a fleshly body in my womb, my own life became alight with Nurturance and other teachings from the Beloved Mother of God who was reminding me of the ways I had forgotten because of my worldly life. She was spiritually nursing me so that I would remember the mother I am in my spirit being form:

> *Daughter, you were rushed so quickly from destruction and death, unto resurrection and Life, and to be Gifted the precious responsibility of bringing forth Life anew ... How utterly and unfathomably awesome! Breathe in this gift of God's Body unto your own. Make this the Nourishment that you feed the babe growing within you. Keep his memory clear about who he really is and to Whom he really belongs.*

She spoke to me with waves of warm tingles, and my interpretations of her presence in energy became as clear as a mountain spring during my daily quiet sitting meditations. Holding my necklace of the Virgin Mary with my left thumb and index finger became my symbolic way of tuning in to her when I was ready to listen and Receive more guidance and whatever wisdom she saw fit to shine upon me. Little did I know that those sweet and quiet moments of intention to hear her would turn into something much more majestic in the months and years to come.

I shall not jump too far forward, however, for it is a cold Winter's night, and cold Winter nights require the mirroring of the Trees in their restful dormancy, a going inward toward the Root of the matter.

Let me slow down and offer you this next story as if I am handing you a warm cup of hot chocolate, or a cup of cinnamon tea, if you prefer that, as we sit in front of a perfect hearth fire on this frosty January eve. I shall relate the next wave of my experience in just such a fashion, weaving in and out of time, like the rising steam from your cup as you sit here with me. I am speaking directly to your timeless spirit, and in so doing, making God's Healing crystal clear for every cell of your body and every wave of your mind. Breathe deeply, my friend, blow on your cup as the steam rises. This is an act of Faith! Rejoice in the awareness that your own Healing is intertwined with my true stories. *Praise God!* The warmth of the tea makes one feel so complete, so cozy and loving. Who would think that a little cup such as this could make one feel so whole?

Yes, it was I myself who made the commitment to Wholeness, back when I was still in the eating disorder rehab program. But I had nothing to do with the miracle of my menstrual flow coming back so quickly. Nothing at all. I was shocked that December day of 2000, to have been so devoid of life for so long, and then to see that precious blood emanating from my flesh once again. No words, no amount of Prayer are sufficient to express the rays of Gratitude I felt then and now for the miracles that have and continue to pour forth.

I was not intending to become pregnant anytime soon at that time. I had doubts about my boyfriend's lifelong commitment to me, even though I never would have voiced that at the time. I really believed my mind to be so askew and tender, so in need of Renewal. Since I was just getting back on my feet in a functional way, how could I entertain in a willful manner, the requirements and obligations of Motherhood? How could I possibly take care of another being, when I was myself in such need of nurturing?

Having a functional brain and cognition was also so very fresh at that point. God had Healed my ability to finish sentences, to think coherent thoughts, to mentally process things again while I was in the hospital. But it was not the cognitive therapy sessions with the rehab psychologist that did anything for me. God had another method, which He put into action through me.

Painting and drawing had become a means by which I could express when things were still disconnected in my mind. Art was a way out of my conscious mind—a mind that wouldn't make the electrical bridges of light translate into anything understandable. Yes, I thought of it as a way out, but more importantly it was the way for God to get in. (I truly know that the Holy Spirit works through artistic expression, and I strongly encourage you and all those you care about to seek the form of creativity that best suits the soul, when in need and beyond.)

There was a mystery, a sublime radiance that took over my flesh and conscious mind when I picked up the colored pastels and crayons and took to the drawing board. Colors and cosmic shapes made sense to me, in contrast to the words of the blabbering therapist who encouraged us inpatients to repeat positive affirmations, empty words, that had no cornerstone within me. As my old passion for singing was lying deep in hibernation—partly, I am sure, because my thinking was so severed—God found another way to create through me. The colors of visual art streamed forth from my soul and spirit onto paper, by way of God's Love. All those hues and shades began to speak to my heart with clarity, while stilling the whole of my being so that God's Hand could miraculously heal my brain, heart, and reproductive system. What a mess He had to work with, but what BEAUTY He brought forth through my hands unto those endless sheets of sketch paper!

At first, the colors just merged and flowed into each other with no direct obvious imagery. I would just pick up any pastel or crayon and take flight. My eyesight had also suffered because of the anorexia, and if I was not wearing my eyeglasses, everything was viewed as one gigantic blob of blur. It frustrated me ever deeper, considering the state of my mind. I wanted to see in a different way. I wanted to take that blindness and find some new eyes.

I became addicted to this healthy, creative pursuit, and I decided to try something new. I began the amazing activity of drawing with a handkerchief fully covering my eyes. Remember, I was not thinking very clearly, and I had no conscious intention or forethought about the art other than a curiosity to observe, when finished, what would come out. It became intriguing, exciting, and novel in such a way I had not felt since my childhood days. It was good JOY medicine, but at the same time, my ego told me that the activity was just a frustrated acceptance of the fact that so much of me felt like it was just "gone," so what did I have to lose in blindly drawing nonsense?

Then another Miracle came forth. The more I drew, the more I noticed faint images that made sense to me after I took off the handkerchief. The most striking and wondrous was that of the shape of a baby, floating in a starry sky-scape. The first time I observed this image was after one of my "blind" drawings. During that particular session—and I always did this art by myself during "quiet time" in the rehab—I felt unusually hopeful, spritely even, and my drawing hand danced across the page with unbridled glee. 20 minutes later, I ripped off the handkerchief and stared in awe. The image of the baby had an umbilical cord connected to a huge bright star, and there was even the indication that it was a boy. My breath quickened.

I was reminded in that moment with a crystal-clear visual of my boy-Child, who had visited me in my darkest hour three years prior. This was HOPE made manifest, and I know that the spirit of my son was in conjunction with the workings of the Holy Spirit through that art and ever more.

Wake UP, Mommy! I am coming! I am coming when you least expect it!

Indeed he did.

When I confirmed my pregnancy, just two months after my womb was Healed, it was Valentine's Day of 2001.

No Greater Love than what God provides. *Alleluia!*

Those nine months were filled with the nourishment and nurturance for not just the wee one inside, but for my whole mind, body, heart, and soul. I intentionally stayed away from books about pregnancy, as I desired my dedication to God through Nature to be my greatest teacher. I was not actively reading the Holy Bible at that time in my life, but gardening and sleeping under the stars was part of my daily Prayer way to the Holy Spirit. I was driven to speak to the Ancestors, and identity with my Filipino and Lakota blood lines motivated my desire to communicate with my spirit family in heaven, particularly any Grandmothers whose messages I might be able to feel in my heart. I wanted their direct radiance to shine through my mind and body, for the sake of my star baby. I wanted so badly to be a GOOD Mother, and felt confident that nine months would give me at least a brief space of time to listen and learn what I could.

Starry, Starry Heavens! Staring endlessly at the Pleiades in those last days of Winter in 2001, was my favorite nightly activity. My wonderment of where my son's spirit had been residing all this "time" before coming down to little old me, on this Earth was delightful. I wondered both quietly and out loud, talking to my baby and asking him questions, singing to him, playing my favorite classical composers through headphones positioned on my belly, for him ... and for the Healing.

And yes, I was 100% sure my baby was a "he." Part of my impatience and my back and forth between a raw and natural pregnancy and allopathic ways, was such that I got an ultrasound when my gestation was 15 weeks along. Clear as day, my baby had positioned himself perfectly to let it be VERY clear that he was indeed, a beloved he. In fact, his arrangement was so overt, the ultrasound image looked like he was deliberately and strategically posing for the shot. It was him saying, "Look, Mommy, you gotta get it straight that I am who I am. Believe it!"

Believe it I did, and somehow, all the pain of the past seemed to just evaporate, to just be gone with purity, not mental contrivance as it had been before. Now, all of the inhales I had concentrated on in sitting meditations for my own Healing needs, were focused upon this wee one. I had someone to offset my former rigid and self-centered existence because of, and by way of, his own life. I had the grand responsibility of growing in God as my boy was growing inside me. There was nothing else I wanted to do other than to be a Good Mother for him, and to be all the things for his own proper spiritual Reminders, which I had so badly needed as a Child. This pregnancy was finally re-tuning me in to the Reality that Life was so much greater than even the beautiful confines of Nature on Earth and the circumstances of this worldly life. I was determined to become what God intended for me, so that I would live my part perfectly for the WHOLE of God's Life, not just for life on this planet. This spirit being baby had been sent by God to remind me ever deeper and higher of exactly who I am in this Infinity, and to assist in

God's Great Plan in such a way that I was unable to see exactly at age 24.

After nine months of Prayer in solitude, Prayer in the preparation and drinking of herbal teas, Prayer in gardening, Prayer in Yoga, Prayer in innocent wonder of our God; after the 42 hours of labor at home on a cold and rainy November evening, after hours of exhaustion, Singing, and sweat, my baby was born powerfully and perfectly into the warm and heavenly waters of a bathtub at home.

Praise God!

Two years and ten months later, my second Child was born in that same bathtub, in the same house as that of her brother's birth. Her emergence into this Earthly part of God's Plan was far swifter, far less dramatic, and even more powerful. Laboring for only three hours as opposed to 42, I meandered in the night-blessed Gardens on the land where I lived on that Indian summer night, listening to the orchestral serenades of the stars, the crickets, and the plants, as my womb contracted while my Baby breathed the celestial nutrition of my indomitable love for her.

Through my listening and observation, I came to remember that there is a totally unique energy in becoming pregnant within differing seasons. My son was conceived at the tail end of Winter, and my daughter was conceived at the tail end of Fall. The positioning of the Earth in relation to the Sun and stars of this galaxy does have direct physiological effect on the baby and mother's body. Additionally, the seasonal energy of the Earth most assuredly affects the soul of the mother and how she relates to the Gift inside her. Fall is the season where

Gratitude is strong in the enjoyment of the year's harvest. It is the time when the fires are lit and the nights are longer, in preparation for the crisp Winter evenings when God's Love is kindled ever brighter from the inside out. In Winter, all the roots are sleeping, deeply cradled in the Earth's womb, and this season of White is the purity which provides the opportunity to go inward and deeper into the stuff of life that really matters, a time for introspection. These were the energies that my soul was given in my Return to Motherhood and the secrets of Infinite Life.

My sacred daughter, this precious growing baby, revealed much mystery as her body grew in my womb. She was a spirit being of incredible power, and she wanted me to know of it by way of the radiance she sent forth through that pregnancy. Her part of God's Great Plan was so blessedly different from her brother's purpose, indeed. I had already seen her twice in spiritual vision, along with her siblings, but I was amazed to discover her unique communion with Nature and her degree of power over it, while in utero. Here's an excerpt from my journal describing this awesome observation:

May 09, 2004

Something wild has been happening for a few days now, and today was the cherry on the cake. I am so glad I have NOT gotten an ultrasound to see you, baby Girl, because I do not need that and you do not need that either. I know who you are! Ok ... WOW! How did you do that? When we were in the Garden today in my usual Prayer sit up against the Oak, in total stillness I asked you to show me which of these early spring herbs you were most drawn to, which ones you knew best, and the very moment after that thought emerged, Almond, our little gray cat, trotted over to the Red Clover patch, ripped a few flowers with her teeth, and pranced over to me, dropping the precious floritas in my lap! I was astonished but not surprised, and as I stared upon the hundreds of tiny florets upon the stem, you kicked so hard in affirmation.

My own dense mind needs those kicks, Baby! Don't you ever stop reminding me of everything I have forgotten, ok? I adore you, little Girl of Heaven ... so then I asked you what your most favorite Animals are. The words "on Earth" kept repeating in my mind, and in that next minute Noah's Ark seemed to have let loose upon our little homestead. Flocks of birds came swooping into the garden, three dogs from neighboring lands appeared some 50 feet away combined with a cacophony of barking dogs from farther in the distance, five cats jumped across the tomato Garden fencing, and three bunnies seemed to have popped out of the ground all at once ... all of this quicker than the flash of an eye, so it seemed. I was half-expecting an Elephant and a Lion to come lumbering around the corner of the house and a Dolphin to jump out of the Water fountain! I got the message very clearly that your adoration for ALL Animals was like no other, dear Precious Baby Girl! Oh, how much FUN we will have when you are here with your brother!

My daughter truly was her own embodiment of Christ's Healing, and soon after she was born, I made two major decisions that propelled me in God's Healing and the constant uplifting of my soul within His Faith. The first was the lesser of the two, in that I finally made the choice to proceed with a much needed surgery on my jaw. Nine years before the birth of my daughter, when I was 18, I had been told by a dentist that three of my four wisdom teeth had grown in horizontally, and that this would continue to cause havoc to my well-being because of the constant pain that would be unavoidable. The pressure of the rooted teeth, and their inability to emerge fully because of their positioning, would push my other teeth uncomfortably, and would place a constant and severe stress on all the nerves in my jaw. He explained to me that these nerves are directly linked to my spine and to my brain's electrical circuitry, and that if I wanted to do something good for myself, that moment in time was the best for me to get those teeth removed.

Well, my mother told me that he was just trying to suck a couple grand from me, coming up with a reason to get me under his knife.

I know clearly that the physical torment of living with such horrid and constant strain upon my nervous system contributed to my suicidal depression and was very much a part of the reason why I wanted to leave my body. Two years after that helpful dentist gave me his diagnosis is when I killed myself.

But it took nearly 10 more years for me to finally decide to do what needed to be done, and have the so-called "wisdom" teeth extracted. In those 10 years, and even after my clear decision to fully reject the minions of evil in the hell of self-destruction, I had learned how to cope, barely, with the constant pressure, the constant grinding stress of my head feeling as if it was lodged between two tight steel walls.

With my newborn perfect baby girl nursing at my breast, staring into her enormous, bright Brown eyes, I told her, "You, *mi Rosita pequenita*, (my Little Rose) will be my helper in this. I am going to pump lots of my milk for you, and you will have to drink it from a bottle for awhile because the doctor will have to give me drugs to knock me out while he cracks open my jaw. But I have to get these things out. It will help me be a better Mommy for you and your brother."

The surgery took three hours, as the micro-facial surgeon had to cut through my gums, use an orthodontic jack saw of sorts to hammer through the back of my mouth on three different sides, and then dig out all the loose pieces of tooth that were so deeply wedged into my gums. In the consultations prior to the surgery, I had told him that I would not accept any post-surgery pain killing medications because I had a breast-feeding four month old at home.

His response was, "Umm, that's nice, but when you come out of what I have to do to your face, you are going to want all the pain killing you can get."

When the surgery was complete, and as the effects of the anesthesia began to wear off, I had never felt such lightning and streaming pain. EVER. The pain was a searing, pulsing and jagged bolting energy that filled my whole head, and pummeled down through my spine and back up again. One family member said he could even see my jaw pulsing.

Perhaps I was being a martyr, but I stuck true to what I had told that surgeon. I left the prescription for painkillers on his desk, and went home to my baby. I was concerned about the purity of my breast milk for my daughter, and I also steadfastly committed to acting on my Faith in God's Healing. I knew this was going to be big, but I did not know HOW big it would get.

For the first week, in the rare moments when I was not holding and nursing my baby, I cried into my pillow so that my toddler son could not hear or see me. When I held my sweet angel girl to my breast, I rocked and rocked, singing Song after Song after Song to ride along with the pain. She must have thought she was on a boat or something, for the only activity I could do to maintain composure was to rock back and forth, back and forth, HUMMING and Singing my heart out to God.

I am a master improvisational Singer of His Heavenly Rays. God has continued to increase this ability so that now I have the sacred gift of specific Healing Song-creation that I share with mankind by way of the Bliss-Parsons Institute and my ongoing production of recorded music. But in those moments of Christ's Healing Fire, when I was at the peak of vulnerability and tender sensitivity in my nervous system, my spirit was able to clutch my soul and body fully and completely by way of the HUM through my Song.

Through the FIRE of that painful Healing, I was Reborn and Returned once again. The reception, transmission, and radiation of The HUM was becoming stronger through me than it ever was, even when I was a small child.

I had thought that giving birth to my sacred spirit being children was powerful! After their births, I truly thought that there could be no greater thing that God would do through my life. How little did I know!

It took nearly two months for the pain to be completely lifted from my being, in the settling in of my jaw. After that first week, I chose to immerse myself in dance and Song, sitting meditations, Yoga, and exercise as physicalized Prayer. I became a fanatic with regard to the study of herbs and nutrition. I knew that I was building my spiritual muscles, and I wanted my flesh to reflect the passionate Love I felt for God's Life, for my Holy Creator, Savior, Redeemer, Healer and ONE True Parent.

I knew what the next greatest activity of Faith and Healing would be for me, the very moment that my nervous system and jaw were Healed. While I was working in the Garden with my toddler son by my side and my baby girl wrapped in a sling, I declared to God that I intended to be healed of my legally blind eyesight.

When I was 11 years old I saw an optometrist for the first time because I was having difficulty seeing things at a distance. He told me that the shape of the retinas in both eyes was such that my condition of near-sightedness would only worsen, year by year. He said that by the time I was 24, I very well might not be able to see anything more than light without any form.

Corrective lenses were a part of my growing into adulthood, as my eyesight did indeed worsen over those years, but I came to know that the outcome was not to be as predicted. The resurrection from suicide, the birthing of both my babies at home, and the Healing of the lightning stress within my bones and nervous system had brought me to the full realization of the Power of God's Healing, Mercy, and Majesty. I knew the next journey, the Healing of my vision, would surely come to pass. My Faith was bigger than this universe, and increasing at an exponential rate because of God's Grace alone.

Mysterious things begin to happen when God can see the truth of a heart when it comes to an expressed dedication in Prayer. He had been waiting for that moment when I got on my knees in the Garden, sank my fingers into the dirt, and wiped it on my eyelids. I had remembered the passage from the Holy Bible when Jesus took some clay into His Hands and used it to bless the eyes of the blind man unto restored sight. I wanted that same communion of experience, and I wholeheartedly believed I would Receive it in full. The following passage is taken from my journal entry of June 27, 2005:

Precious Creator,

I want so badly in this moment to be Healed in my vision. There is so much that I have tried to hide from, and I know that part of why I am blind is because I did not want to see the world around me, as a child. I want to SEE with 20/20 vision, and far beyond this as well. I know it is Your Will to Heal me in full, and I need You to wash strength, patience, and focus in this path of Your Power. I have no idea how long this will take, but I give all of me to You, in this specific Prayer.

Thank you, Lord!

Back then, I had not yet remembered how to CLAIM God's Healing for myself, but I knew His Healing power very well. And indeed, it was a very smart thing for me to have Prayed in request of strength, patience, and focus for the path ahead of me, as I so very much needed the patience!

Intertwining is God's Medicine, weaving and breaking through the boundaries of the flesh, the mind, and time. Motherhood of two wee ones was my biggest teacher in patience, so the answer to that part of my Prayer was already in evidence, and then some. Coincidingly, on the very same day that I wrote that journal entry, I accidentally stepped on my only pair of eyeglasses and crushed them into oblivion. It was an unintentional move, but I recognized that God was telling me that the best way for me to begin to Receive His Healing for my eyes, was to only see as I could see in that moment of time.

What I quickly discovered was that I had made myself blind. But one of the sweetest journeys of Reuniting with the HUM was the strengthening bond between my soul and my spirit, as I began to really see what lay at the root of my blindness.

Nothing is an accident in God's Life, and the synchronicity of happenings became fascinating to me.

In that first week of dedication to the Healing of my sight, I walked to the local library with my son in a stroller and my baby in a sling. I wanted to find a book on the physiology of human eyeballs and how they are arranged in relation to the brain and nervous system. I thought that by learning about the structure of the eyes I could use visualization, combined with the HUM, in order to accelerate my physiological response to God's Rays. This was a healthy intention, but God had another plan.

When I got to the shelf where I knew I could find the book I was looking for, I bent forward to see the names on the labels of the books. I was wearing my sleeping baby daughter in a sling. All of a sudden, she jolted from her nap with a strange and happy burst of awakening. Her sudden squirming startled me, jolting me upright in response. The result was that I banged my head on one of the bookshelves. Well, only one book fell off that shelf, and it was not a book on the anatomy of the eyes.

It was a book that triggered my spiritual knowing that vision entails far more than just the light passing through the cornea, hitting the retina, stimulating rods and cones, and traveling through the optic nerves. It was not written from a strictly physiological viewpoint, but it was a spiritual and soulful analysis of why eyesight becomes challenged. What I read started a Fire that burned through the whole of my being. After only 10 pages I needed to read no more. I returned it to the library the next day, and began the undoing of my blindness within the Power and Might of Jesus Christ.

I focused my vision on the flame of a candle twice each day for 30 minutes in the morning and 30 minutes at night before bed. The more I focused on that single flame, the more my perceptual vision changed. My sight began to soften, and at first I could see only a growing space within the center of the flame. Then, my focus brought forth the ability to make that one flame into two, then three, then four flames within my field of vision. I decided not to make things too complicated and restrained myself from allowing my sight to see with more than two flames.

I questioned this, wondering why I could see this way, but only with attention and concentration. My questioning was silenced, as my spirit answered, saying, "Because I am remembering what Truth vision really looks like as the spirit I am, and I must be patient, as I am in this physical body."

Sometimes, the space in the middle of the candle appeared as a sort of crystal. I would be completely attuned to the inhale and exhale of my oceanic spirit Breath, and after thanking God for the precious Healing activity (as was my habitual custom) a movie roll from my past would appear. It was not as if I saw miniature people inside the candle, but as my perception tuned into the candle flame, a broad expanse of orange light would open, like a widening tunnel between myself and the flame. There I saw episodes from my past when evil energies from others challenged my attunement and communion in the HUM. I saw myself running and hiding in the bathroom and under the bed's blankets. I saw my daddy's screaming face, my mother asleep from exhaustion on the couch, and my sister crying. I saw things exploding and breaking against walls. And then the image would just be over.

After about three sessions of this, I realized that God was telling me that I had not yet let go completely of all the residue of stuffed evils. I had not truly come to embody the SPIRIT of CHRIST'S FORGIVENESS for all the other people in my life, nor had I given myself Christ's Love. As a result, and most importantly, I had not fully given the whole of my being back to CHRIST alone.

As you recall, I was first given the sacred Gift of Motherhood only four years after being brought back from the dead, and was blessed with a second child two years and ten months later. Even though I was truly devoted to living life Renewed and whole in happiness and health, I had not done the proper work of fully letting go of the past. Becoming blinded was my soul's way of dealing with an uncleansed mind.

Again, I was on my knees in awe of all that God was giving me in the Healing, each day recording in my journal the realizations brought by these endless discoveries.

Oh, and there were tears. Deluges of tears flowed forth for many weeks, as I was finally releasing my soul from the bondage of years of childhood and young adulthood spent in total hell. Memories came to me during sleep-side dreams and during my waking hours, working in the Garden with the babies.

Evil frequencies lodged as stuffed negative emotions run deep into the subconscious mind and flesh. They all began to bubble up, one by one, and the minions of evil took great pleasure, as they were energetically made aware that the negative waves of rage and hurt were still trying to breathe inside my mind and heart. If that sounds crazy to you, read that last sentence again. It is true. The minions of evil are very much aware when their fuel, which is all energy waves of anything negative, is made manifest through anyone, anywhere. It is exactly what gives them life to mutate and to feed off other people and other situations no matter where in the world a person is. Remember, the butterfly effect is such that what one thinks and does, ripples outward into the Life with no limitations. God's Life in all universes is an open space of ENERGY.

I was determined not to let those nasty lies have one more breath, but it was a very difficult and challenging exorcism.

The fascinating thing was, that when the Holy Spirit could see that I had truly let go of a particular aspect of the abuse and neglect, my physical eyesight would improve! I was slowly beginning to see things more clearly. I was my own witness in this at first. I drew words on ten different sheets of paper and randomly shuffled the papers, pulling out one to tape to the wall. Every day,

I would change the paper, so as to not memorize the words, relying on that as a way to recognize the letters. I marked the spot on the floor at the point where I could see all the words perfectly and clearly. Slowly, that piece of tape on the hardwood floor got further and further away from the wall with the taped words. *Praise God!*

As my babies were getting bigger, my spirit was becoming the dominant controller of my whole being. I knew my spirit was in communion with Christ. I KNEW I belonged to God alone, and I just sailed along with my ever-increasing clarity of vision. When Jesus could see that I had REALLY Returned to the true essence of Forgiveness, which is the embodiment of GIVING the whole mind, the whole heart, and the whole body unto Him alone, my eyesight was completely restored.

In the span of 4 years, from 2004 to 2008, my eyesight was healed by 8 ¾ diopters. I knew this after I had gone back to an optometrist for a check up exam. When he asked me when I had had my LASIK surgery, my response was "Oh, God does not use lasers. That method won't help anyone really see. Lasers will just correct one kind of vision, and I have always wanted far more than THAT." He had no idea what I was talking about. He just shrugged his shoulders, told me what my current diopter reading was, and walked out of the room. I smiled and pranced out of the building.

So, in this year of 2015 I am far from being legally blind. My vision is not 20/20, but it is pretty darn close. And I am certainly not required to wear glasses while driving. I do not wonder why God has not taken me over the edge into perfect worldly vision, because I am clearly seeing and living Truth.

The supernatural perception and attunement that has returned to my consciousness is sweeter, more vivid, more alive, and more exciting than having eyeballs that are 100% in the functioning of my rods and cones.

I have dutifully stayed my course in Christ's Healing and my work within God's Will via the ministry, which consumes my life daily. I claim His Healing for my whole being in my every waking and sleeping moment, and intertwinedly, this means that I claim His Healing for ALL who are in need; all 7 billion residents of planet Earth.

God's Healing Showers are endless. How much deeper and wider will you open, so as to Receive for yourself and for the whole of mankind? Yes, the Rays of God's Will as the Healing are invisible and more powerful than anyone can possibly imagine, and the manifestations of His Healing often seem to appear out of nowhere.

Appearing out of nowhere—that's how God works the Healing. It's happening all of the time, involuntarily cascading upon the whole of life on Earth, invisible to human eyes in Its Divine cosmic frequencies.

People wonder why they are not healed of this or that. People doubt so vehemently, and many people flat out reject God *in toto*. Yet the ones who may be interested in or craving the Healing are unwilling to accept that they are the very ones who are cutting themselves off from it!

God's Healing is more real than anything and everything that can be seen with the human eye, and I treasure it as the shimmering cascade of His Infinite Power that it is. I love upon and within its transmission for all Life on this planet, as this is part of my Assignment and has been for millions of years.

I am both a physical mother unto three most precious and eternal spirit being children (the third of whom is not yet in body), and a Mother of God's Will in the Nurturing radiance of Creator's HUM for all who would Receive Him. The intertwining reality of my physical and spiritual Motherhood is central to my being—always has been, and always will be.

I tell you, there is nothing more real to confirm one's place in God's Might and Love than a wanted pregnancy and Motherhood. There is no other experience a soul can have on Earth, which offers such an opportunity to taste of God's Life, than through the magic of having another spirit being take form, through one's own flesh. There is no greater experience that reminds a soul of the interconnectivity of all Life, no matter what the universe, than what Motherhood intrinsically offers in its essence. But how many women on this planet really understand this and live in this kind of joy? This is not a world in which anybody can truly feel safe, even in one's own home. People's natural inclination is not to know themselves as spirit beings living a spiritual life, but to pursue having a life while encumbered with the manifestations of religious, social, and political abuses and murder that abound around the globe. Motherhood, both physical and spiritual, is a gift of God's Healing given to many beings for the purpose of Healing the whole of mankind. It is up to one more individual on Earth who truly Adores Christ to take this truth a step further.

Physically, Motherhood pertains to females who are given the gift of reproduction in body, and there are specific and obvious responsibilities a woman has in the proper raising of a child born through her. But spiritual

Motherhood is what I want to describe and clarify, as it is an energy and radiation of God's Will which goes beyond all things of life on Earth. It is spiritual Motherhood that is the core essence of my ministry of Christ's Healing, which was born at the time of my own son's birth approximately 13 years ago.

Today His ministry through me is entitled Voice of Christ's Healing, but in the beginning it had no name. It has been activated beyond time, however, and it was organic in its evolution on Earth. God will always put disciples in the exact settings in which their gifts are best utilized. As Motherhood became my given path, the Holy Spirit drew other young mothers into my life who were in need of a friend to assist them in pregnancy and childbirth. Ten years later, I found myself looking back on a space of time in which I had actually served as a doula and traditional lay midwife, sometimes traveling hundreds of miles to assist a woman in delivery of her baby. My years spent Reconnecting with herbs, living in Nature, and truly loving other mothers, combined with understanding the rhythms of pregnancy and my own child-birthing, giving me some amount of knowledge and wisdom which I was then able to share with over 100 women in that 10 year space of time.

My own service to pregnant women was always free of charge, and for the first ten births I attended, there was not even barter in exchange for the time, energy, and support I shared with those women, their babies, and their families. I had no regrets, for I loved the work. I rejoiced in seeing a woman discover a new ray of power and Healing in bearing forth her baby at home. Fortunately—Praise God—nearly all of the births I attended had positive outcomes. I was blessed to bear witness to the healthy and happy manifestation of God's Miracle of Life, over and over. Then I began to realize something about the nature of my midwifery work and of the women I was called forth to assist. It was something that began to taste spiritually sour.

As I watched each woman become radiantly happy after overcoming what seemed like very trying circumstances in the birth of her baby, I began to see a common thread: there was no real Praise and Glory being given to God Alone. Yes, it was indeed beautiful to see a woman get over her personal demons sufficiently to allow the power of God's Gift to bring forth a healthy baby at home. This is precious in its own right as the woman usually came to a healthier place about being a soul. What I was NOT seeing was the woman being born into the understanding of herself as an eternal spirit being belonging to God Almighty alone. There was no rejoicing in mysterious awe of God's Majesty and gracious gifting by way of another successful and safe birth, with baby drinking breast milk in the sanctity of the home. It all seemed to be about the mother, the "mother goddess"—expressively worshipped by many of them over God Almighty, Who was thought of as a "man" and therefore unworthy of their adoration—and how powerful she had become in and of her own might and focus through that birth.

I began to leave each birth with a sense of grieving even though I was truly happy for the woman, her baby, and family, because the focus was not wholly in the ONE God. Something was just not right. I came to realize that the circle of women in which I had been serving had a feminist and self-centered spirituality about their consciousness rather than a HOLY SPIRIT-filled consciousness.

God is no respecter of persons, because a person is a thing of this disconnected world. God craves that all who are called would CHOOSE to know that they are one in Creator alone, and gifted with ALL the promises of Jesus the Christ, Who IS a Man and God made Manifest. This does not mean that a woman, or a man, should develop a spiritual ego the size of New York, because they think they are "divine" in and of themselves or because they have been graced with a healthy home-birth, but this is the collective mindset I was observing, and it just was not for me.

I wanted Jesus' Mind and Heart to radiate through my own. I wanted the Purity of His Healing to use my life so completely, that the whole of my work, every single thought, and every single word that left my lips was a cosmic ray of Praise and Glory for the ONLY ONE Who possesses ALL Life and all universes. I was re-uniting with my eternal essence in Him. I wanted to see as many people as possible, not just women, come to His Infinite Body by way of their CHOICE to Return to HIS Truth in Healing.

I knew that the Miracles through my life, combined with my gift of writing, speaking, and powerful Singing Voice were the media by which the Holy Spirit was shaping the REAL ministry I was to engage in. The ironic thing is that even when I was still in the space of time attending home births, I was also traveling to these other secular places I have mentioned, testifying to my own powerful Healing stories. The Holy Spirit was weaning me off one branch of service, while activating me in another. It was the latter that started to mean so much more, with such rich spiritual Fruit obviously being born from the presentations I gave at those schools, prisons, and hospitals. How much more powerful to bear Witness in body, to 25 inmates about the Power of Renewal in Christ over and above watching a woman glorify her own soul in childbirth?

Slowly, the Holy Spirit's weaning cut off my service to women in childbirth, and I began to devote my midnight hours (as my days were reserved for providing for and tending to my own children) to co-authoring books with Dr. DH Parsons, a former evangelical minister and President of the Bliss-Parsons Institute. I myself became Associate Vice-President of B-PI, which is an organization devoted to supporting and radiating the Truth of God in its various manifestations by way of science, art, music, some religions, Yoga, the studies of Health and well-being, and self-realization. I chose to align myself with B-PI and work for it. I also became immersed in Scriptural Song, coming to write, arrange, record, and produce powerful Healing music, all of which is available to the world at large. After 12 years of traveling to present and singing for people in secular settings, it has only been in the last year that God Almighty Guided me to present in actual church congregations.

"Voice of Christ's Healing" is the name given to this ministry, and it stays as such, no matter what group I am bearing Witness to, no matter how many people choose to Return to the supernatural Divinity of The ONE God's Truth through the work of it, and no matter how many stones may be thrown along the way. The activation of God's Will is all that matters.

Are you ready to get real about what it takes to become a body of Christ's Infinity?

***

BECOMING A BODY OF INFINITY

REQUIREMENTS FOR THE JOURNEY OF HEALING, ACCORDING TO GOD'S WILL:
1. Honesty
2. Daily moments of Stillness and Quietude
3. Attention to Breath/exercise
4. Prayerful conversation with God
5. Expression
6. Dedication
7. Diligence
8. Determination
9. Devotion to God in every moment
10. Patience

Do you realize that the number one barrier to your becoming a body of Christ's Infinity is your own resuscitation of the evil energy that Christ destroyed for you and all mankind? Your entrenched addictions to the lies of this false-faced world, as well as your own negative emotional thinking is the very fuel of addiction to ego, and THIS is of your own creation.

You have spent years forming an identity as a human being, perhaps following the doctrine of a particular religion, perhaps even really believing that you know God's Will. But I know that the majority of people on this planet do not have one clue about the Supernaturally Divine Healing Power of Jesus Christ. I am absolutely confident that if you do not CHOOSE to Renew the WHOLE of your mind in Christ—no matter how long it takes for you to fully accept that he has FULLY cleansed you from the bondages of dis-ease, death, and the wages of sin—you will continue to feed the evil that is currently wiping mankind from this world. You ARE the problem if you remain stuck, for one more moment of this most precious Life of Christ's, by your own disinterest, lack of commitment, or disbelief in the Healing Radiance of the ONE God Almighty.

A Good Mother speaks harshly in Truth, as needed.

One thing I observe in people beginning their path of Renewal in Christ is the back and forth of emotional trauma they put themselves through. Doubt, guilt, anger, envy, lust, jealousy, hatred, depression, anger, rage, and excessive sorrow all fester in the subconscious mind of EVERY PERSON ON THIS PLANET, and each of these frequencies of the minions of evil will surface in the conscious mind of the one who is making the choice to Return to Christ.

Why? Why is it so difficult, the moment a person is truly crushed in a taste of God's Love and Truth and Might? For that is what one Receives in the moment God sees that the mind and heart are unified in the expression of repentance and display of humility. You have to get on your knees in one way or another and be BROKEN from the bond of lies created by you in these short years of your worldly life. That glorious moment of being crushed in the Realization of Repentance and the Acknowledgement that Jesus' Blood was shed for your Salvation will be challenged in the very next hour, and for the weeks, months, and years to come if you do not put on the warrior armor of Truth with every single breath.

I am speaking literally here. Know this: The devil is defeated, yes, and even the worst preacher on the planet professes this, but his minions are alive and well and will feed off you with a vengeance as you exorcize the lies from the deepest recesses of your own mind. One day you will feel on top of the world because you woke up after your Rebirth in the Holy Spirit, and all of a sudden, one of those negative emotions rears up in some life circumstance, to make you doubt your Salvation in Christ. Its parasitic force works because those dead lies feed off of your own soul and heart. Jesus shakes His Head in grief, every single day as He observes the individual and collective minds of mankind.

Here are examples of some of those lie-ridden voices of ego addictions:

I am still doing it! I am still reacting in the same way whenever he says that to me. Lord, I have given this to you over and over, but it still won't leave me alone!

I cannot get rid of my jealousy of her. She does not deserve what she's got. I am the one who worked so hard to get there, but I am still here.

I am this way because of what my father did to me when I was a child.

When the lies of the past and satan's manifestation of negative emotional addiction are allowed to remain in your conscious mind for even just one moment, you allow God's ceaseless Healing rays to be BLOCKED. You cut yourself off from the manifestation of His Promises, made in the Kingdom of God, in your life here and now. Your body remains plagued with this infestation of evil and it leads to accelerated physical aging, a compromised immune system, deficient red blood cells, inflammation, or perhaps the beginning of cancer—to name just a few possible physical effects brought on by years of harboring lies. Your body becomes doomed in and of this world because of a mind that will not succumb and yield to the Omnipresence of the Body, the Light, the Truth, and Heart of God Almighty.

What's the solution? What are the actual practices and ways you can adopt as your own that will fully Renew the whole of your life, and thereby propel you into Becoming a Body of Christ's Infinity?

The above list of 10 requirements is the very substance of the Warrior armor you must wear as well as the Sword of Christ you will bear, while living in this world. Evil has many faces and forms in this increasingly hell-focused world and one must protect oneself and one's children, but your biggest enemy is what lies hidden in the darkest parts of your mind. When you fully rid yourself of those illusory lies, then you are really wielding the Sword of Christ, assisting the Holy Spirit in bringing cleansing to this whole world, person by person.

We are now going to cast clarifying light on each of the 10 requirements for the journey in Healing. Before we begin, I want to stress that these requirements of Becoming a Body of Infinity, are not isolative, nor are they to be accomplished as separate and individual steps. They are continuous rays—continuous frequencies similar to the spectrum of light when seen as a rainbow—that must be reflected upon and implemented into the daily life interchangeably. I am breaking them down in discussion so that you can meditate upon and observe your own internal life, to see which of these gifts of God's Holy Spirit you need to make an effort to reunite with.

They are all symbiotic in nature, meaning that when you are actively working with one of these, you are immediately nourishing yourself while being lead into another of these required Gifts. The most important thing is that you give your attention and focus to each of them, to ensure that they are all as strong as possible, emanating from your mind and heart and body.

STEP 1: WIELD THE HOLY SPIRIT AS HONESTY

Honesty is not just a quality or virtue. It is not a mental concept or projected thought form. It is not something to be worked at. It is a supernatural frequency that is an exact ray of the Holy Spirit. It is something to unite with and BECOME.

You have spent years lying to yourself regarding your identity and belief systems. You have lived in such a way that you are subject to this world, and this is all entirely egocentric. We have already established the fallacy of the belief that the negative attributes of humanity are part of "human nature." But what happens when you really begin the journey of loving Christ?

After you repent of a wayward past disconnected from Christ, and acknowledge Him as the only Savior, Healer, and Redeemer, your own self-induced "ego-isms" will bubble up from your subconscious mind, persistently working to keep your soul from reconnecting with your spirit. You yourself will cause torment in your own thinking, conscious mind, by allowing all of those stuffed negative emotions from childhood, doubts, insecurities, anger, hurt, etc., to swarm your waking moments, distracting you from the TRUTH that God has already cleansed you of ALL of it. All those sorrowful life moments of your past were transformed into the thick energy frequencies that became patterns of behavior in your life. These behaviors became entrenched over the years as habits, so much so that you came to believe that you are "naturally" hot-tempered, easily depressed, or reclusive when dramatic situations arise, and on and on.

As you realize that it does not feel good to hold on to these ways, you will find yourself Praying to God, asking Him to Heal you of it all, and your ego-born addictions will RAGE upon you even more—they want to be kept alive. These negative emotions, or "ego-isms" as I shall refer to them, are very much a part of how the minions of evil on Earth keep humanity disconnected from the Presence of the Holy Spirit! They are a method of control, so that one more person might die defeated and with an unrepentant heart. The minions of the dead devil are aware that their own master has been vanquished, but they take pleasure in preventing one more soul from returning to the starry heavens from which they originally came. It is their way of "honoring" their defeated master before they themselves are obliterated in the Second Coming, which they very well know is imminent. *Praise God!*

Enter the weapon of HONESTY.

It typically takes a long time for one who has repented to REALLY embody the TRUTH that Jesus Christ did it all in the Atonement of His Blood. With the help of the Ray of the Holy Spirit called HONESTY during that time, the Child of Christ can constantly stay on top of the lingering but dying ego-isms attempting to breathe life through the conscious mind.

Let's get more to the point. My instruction is for those who have already taken that first step in the Return to

Christ's Love in Repentance. As part of that Repentance, you MUST acknowledge, throughout the whole of your being, that you have no personal power of your own, of your own will and accord. You must embody the spirit of humility; that is paramount to Repentance. Whether it takes you one moment or one year or more, it is necessary and VITAL to the rest of your Healing journey in Christ that you do so. If you have not taken this first step, I strongly suggest that you do so immediately by placing yourself meekly before the Majesty of God.

Here is your Golden opportunity. You only have to say it and MEAN it ONCE. When that glorious ripple of elation rocks your body and calms your mind, when you really FEEL the Redemption and Salvation of your life in Jesus the Christ, then take the next steps.

You must become AWARE of when any old thought or ego-ism of the past, creeps into your mind. Honestly announce to the Christ that it is a lie that never belonged to you, and that you cast it into the Living Fire of Christ. Find your own words to say this out loud or internally. Additionally, develop mental image of God's Fire that will, for you, embody the supernatural TRUTH that God destroys the bonds that shackle your being. You need a picture to retrain your mind to obedience and thinking within the Infinite Reality that Christ has already freed you in full.

It is fine to call forth your favorite picture of Jesus, so use one that is a beautiful picture to contemplate as there is immediate Power in His Face and in His Name. If you are able to see His Face the moment that thought of jealousy, hatred, depression, etc., comes to mind, and then are able sense that the ego-ism is immediately gone, then His Face should be the image you stick with. This is not just mental imagining you are doing, and this is NOT a self-help seminar I am teaching. I am REMINDING you of the way your spirit being operates in your TRUE form. Spirit beings exist in the formations of God's Light and communicate with vibratory frequencies that take on wavelengths of form or sound. In bringing forth an image of the Christ's Face, you are embodying His Will of communion with all Life.

For some, the image of Jesus' face does not work so well. For reasons of a personal nature, other images of God's immediate Cleansing are needed. I have suggested, in my own ministry, that the visualization of a Blue Fire is effective. Everyone knows what fire on Earth looks like. It is Orange-Gold hot with a Blue-Violet center, best used for nourishment and heat, but it is an elemental that becomes a dangerous destroyer when it gets out of control. Ask any person to describe the look of fire, and the words and pictures come easily: a singular candle light, licking flames of a campfire, smoke rising, crackling wood, the mesmerizing dance of Orange light brightening up a dark night, etc.

I tell people to turn that easy picture of fire into a BLUE flame because BLUE is God's strongest vibrational current of Healing manifested as color for the benefit of all His children. It is easy to translate the color Blue of the sky, of turquoise, of the ocean waters, or of a pure spring into a FLAME.

Now, combine this with the understanding that your physical body is a powerhouse of fire in its own functioning. Your trillions of cells are constantly dying and being reborn, dying and being reborn. The food you ingest is constantly being burned in the process of metabolism into usable energy. There are trillions upon trillions of electrical charges per second firing across the synapses of your brain. Your FLESH is a creation of God's Living FIRE! Do you see this?

As your mind (which has been composed as your soul), body, and heart are intertwined as one, can you then accept that in belonging to God alone, it is His Fire that consumes you when you choose to Return to Him in full?

See the Blue Flame in those moments when the past seems to haunt you, when you are having that same old reactionary thought or behavior in response to some trying circumstance, when you are despondent and do not know what to do with "how you feel." Let it burn. Let it burn perpetually, using the cleansing Fire of God Almighty, through His Son Jesus, by way of the Holy Spirit in Honesty that none of these thoughts and behaviors are YOU.

Visualization of the Blue Flame all around you and especially within you is a most effective tool used within the Sword of HONESTY. Use this nourishing Fire as much as is needed until you come to that wonderful moment when you accept and realize that you ARE fully freed, cleansed, and Healed. *Praise God!*

STEP 2: DAILY MOMENTS OF STILLNESS AND QUIETUDE
STEP 3: ATTENTION TO BREATH
STEP 4: PRAYERFUL CONVERSATIONS WITH GOD

The next three requirements of Becoming a Body of Infinity are self-explanatory. You simply need to integrate the fact that the only way to truly Receive God's Presence is through daily devotion consisting of any amount of Stillness and Quietude you are willing to create for yourself, attention to the Breath, and ongoing discussions with God Almighty. Truly, all of these tend to happen at once when actively put into practice. Let me explain the nature of these three activities in their individual essences, and what is born forth when they are combined. It is supernatural and most profound.

Stillness and Quietude are considered by many to be the state of non-activity and silence respectively. Most people think that to be still is simply to be not moving. Quietude is associated with not making noise. While these concepts are accurate in an elementary way, I want to expand in God's Truth about what the frequencies of Stillness and Quietude really are.

Stillness and Quietude are waves of spirit energy. One unites with them in order to be made open to Receive the Living Presence of the Holy Spirit. Yes, I said that they are waves of spirit. They are a part of God's Living Body of Light, to which one must Return so that the dross of ego-isms and entrapments of the world can be washed away in the sacred cleansing that comes only through Stillness and Quietude.

As one enters a cave, one can sense the impenetrable Silence that fills the space of it. Ancient beings embodying the spirit of Stillness constitute the rock—beings comprising a combination of minerals, Water, and Earth made solid over millions of years of Earth time. The eternal dance and pervasive force of water has worn away the mass of rock to form the womb of the cave, with all of its mysterious tunneling and irregularities, but the cave as a whole is STILL. Minerals are transported by the slow drip of Water from the ceilings of the cave, taking eons to form the stalactites that hang as rock icicles. The stalactites and their opposing brothers, stalagmites, reside in Stillness within the cave, keeping guard over the sacred presence of God's Stillness there. In caves such as this, God has implanted the energetic stuff that holds this Earth together in one piece. There are mysteries embedded in the sub-atomic structure of everything within that cave, formed and united over the space of eons, so that mankind may come to know and Worship God.

I use this imagery now because I want you to tangibly taste of the spirit of Stillness and to know why it is so important for your own spiritual Return to Infinity.

Your physical body can be compared to that cave. Your flesh is composed mostly of Water, and it was the sacred Water of your biological mother's womb that provided the force which carried nutrients to form your spine, your brain, and the whole structure of your body temple for God's Will. Your body was made from God's Light, translated into Water of and within the womb. It was nourished and structured from the nutrients floating through that Water, and hardened into form in the same way the Water rushed through the mountain to make the cave, carrying forth the minerals to compose its internal structures. Your mother's womb was a place of Quietude, the only sound being the rush of blood—like Water—through her placenta to you, the cave that was being formed.

The sacred difference between you and that cave is that you are one spirit being, converted into the physicality of an ego-shell, or body, who was intended to embody the Will of God in thought, mobility, and consciousness of Christ's Heart. The cave is a spirit being composed of many spirit beings whose job is to radiate the spirit energy of Stillness and Quietude for the benefit of humankind, and in Worship to God Almighty.

You belong to the spirit of Stillness and Quietude, and to see it in this comparative way is most profound, allowing your mind to soften so that the Holy Spirit can teach you more about what you presently are disconnected from. Go deeper into the mysterious cave of your body-being by way of the spirit of Stillness and Quietude.

Devote however many minutes of every morning when you awaken, the very moment you awaken, to a commanded stilling of your body, enjoying the Quietude of the cave of your early morning. If you have the habit of using an alarm clock to begin your day because you feel you need it, then you can simply begin your devotion to God by way of Stillness after you turn it off. I guarantee that the more you practice Stillness in the morning, the less you will rely on the use of an alarm clock. An alarm clock is a glaring obstacle to your unification with Quietude for obvious reasons. You will desire to have those early morning moments with the Christ, and as your spirit starts to become the dominant and real you, the needs of the worldly "you" will begin to dissipate in Truth.

You are not required to sit upright in a cross-legged position and say "OM" to enter the sacred cave of your being where the Holy Spirit will meet you. If you are prone to falling back asleep, then perhaps it might be wise to sit up, propping your back to the wall with pillows. The key here is that you want your very first moments to be given to God completely in the spirit of

Stillness and Quietude. As you enter into these frequencies, the cave of your spirit's exploration will deepen and widen, and you will find yourself craving more of the Holy Spirit. This is your first PRACTICE in Becoming a Body of Infinity now.

Attention to the Breath is the action that should be combined with entering into the cave of your body being. For "you" is not just a place of sanctified darkness on the inside. You are made in the image of God by way of His Fire, and of His Light. Your Breath is the medium the Holy Spirit uses to show you this light, which burns from the inside out, and all around you as well.

You have to have a light with which to see inside your cave, right? Realize that you are a unique spirit being whose light is fully possessed and in communion with God's Light! The deeper you journey into the cave, the stronger your Awareness of this light and the light itself becomes, but only by way of single-minded focus on your inhale and exhale.

Stop reading for a moment and close your eyes. See the deep and mysterious place of what lays hidden within, and BREATHE with loving attention for a count of three inhales and three exhales.

You have just set alight the whole of your body, heart, and soul with the communion of your individual spirit with the Holy Spirit of God.

In the Name of Jesus Christ, you are illuminating your body temple with the new ability to be both a Receiver and Transmitter of God's frequencies—God's Rays and God's Light which are ceaseless and powerful and belong to God alone.

These rays of the Holy Spirit might at first seem to come only in drips, like the Water in the cave. This is because you are just now learning to open yourself to Receive them. In Truth, these Rays of God are streaming ceaselessly from Heaven, all around you, from below, from above, and cascading into the whole of you—who happen to be condensed into that fleshly body temporarily on Earth.

What a holy, holy Gift!

Are you willing to unite with the spirit energy of Stillness and Quietude, daily, so that you may come to know yourself in this way, and more?

What happens when you exit your morning and evening practice of Stillness and Quietude, when you go about the hustle and bustle of your day?

Daily conversations with God are vital, as you engage in your responsibilities and enter into the chaos of the world.

You must tell God that you give the WHOLE of your soul, body, and heart to Him and to Him alone, so that your day begins RIGHT, and so that you will activate and embody the Will of God for your life. When you really mean those words that are the gifting of your being unto He Who Reigns, when you really announce to God that ALL of you is His Possession, your life will reflect the power of the Christ's Indomitable Love that you possess. You will come to think, to speak, to act, and to bring forth aspects of the Kingdom of God in this way. If your conversations with Jesus the Christ are the pathways by which your life is Renewed and all life choices are Guided, then there is only heaven on Earth made manifest for you in His Healing Light, directly affecting all those around you, and the whole of mankind as well.

STEP 5: EXPRESSION
Throughout the process of opening ever deeper, higher, and wider unto Christ, which is what embodying Infinity means, you must also find a means of expression, so that your soul will be able to see what your subconscious and conscious mind is being cleansed of. You will also find that the Holy Spirit is using the expressive activity to further cleanse and nourish you, so that the activity of your personal expression becomes a cathartic energy of cleansing and a catalyst for more nourishing Rays of the Holy Spirit as well, all leading to your place within God's Infinity now.

Whether it be through writing, drawing, modeling clay, embroidery, gardening, woodworking, et cetera, or simply talking to someone who will JUST listen attentively and be a sounding board, you must find a means by which you can express what you are experiencing in this process of Healing that is intrinsic to Becoming a Body of Infinity. Creative expression is also the means by which you maintain the spirit energy of HONESTY, so that as your ego-isms emerge and try to get the best of you, they are put in their place, burned away into the nothing that they are, via the Indomitable Love of God Almighty.

STEP 6: DEDICATION
STEP 7: DILIGENCE
STEP 8: DETERMINATION
STEP 9: DEVOTION
The "four Ds" are intertwining in their unique spirit energies. They exist in God's Body for your benefit, and

for the purpose of assisting you to do God's Will in the present moment. I remind you that I am not discussing these 10 requirements as concepts, as mental choices, or even as attributes of the human character to be attained, but I am teaching the truth that they are energy frequencies, gifts from and of God, which are a necessary part of Returning to the Truth of who you really are in Christ.

There is a popular image of the Christ that I call to your attention here now, for the purpose of clarifying what I mean by this. It is the well-known portrayal of Christ with His right hand held up, and His thumb, index and middle finger held straight and slightly bent forward, but with the ring and pinkie fingers gently pointing downward. He is robed in sacred White, surrounded by His Golden White Glow, and there is a stream of Red and White Rays emanating from His Heart. See this now. If necessary, find a picture of this depiction of Christ, study it, and imprint it into your soul.

Picture the four Ds as these rays, streaming forth from the Heart of Christ, enveloping the whole of your soul, body, and heart. These waves of His own Mind become a part of your very nature because they are aspects of Him. You must wield them like swords, with intention. Study each of them individually to determine how much of each you need to interfuse into your own consciousness. You have to put all of them into practice individually as a way of retraining your mind to understand that you are already freed in Christ.

When you observe in yourself the degree to which you are DEDICATED to God's Will and not your own, the HONESTY of this practice will propel you into choosing positive Truths in place of the dead lies of ego-isms. You are already freed of these, but your conscious mind has not yet accepted the cleansing. Your DILIGENCE and DETERMINATION to be cleansed and Healed will increase because you will desire to continue in this warrior path for God's Will.

Every time you make one move, think one thought that is REALLY born of your soul's communion with your spirit and not your ego, the Holy Spirit washes through you with some new ray of God's Love and Presence, and it feels supernaturally amazing to be cleansed, nourished, and loved in such a way. You apply this to your daily moments, and realize the JOY of belonging to God Almighty alone. This act becomes the embodiment of DEVOTION, which is the frequency, the cosmic ocean, of your Adoration for and of ELOI, the ONE God Almighty, from Everlasting to Everlasting. Again, DEVOTION is the supernatural living ocean that you immerse yourself in, by way of these spiritual discoveries, these gifts and energy frequencies that the Holy Spirit bestows for your Becoming A Body of His Infinity.

As you go along your way in devotion, diligence, determination, now swimming in the ocean of DEVOTION, you will be radiating ALL of these energies to every nano-particle of Life everywhere. No matter where you are physically, and no matter whose presence you are in, your very mind-body-soul will be emanating these gifts because you are now beginning to understand yourself as a spirit being living the Will of God. Your happy countenance will be contagious, and your mere presence will energetically shift any negative frequencies in a room you walk into. Your calm demeanor will be the lamb of Christ soothing everyone inside and out. Your ability to see through the emotional displays of others, with no similar reaction of your own, will be the medium by which the Holy Spirit eradicates more of the negativity from the dimension in which Earth resides, and which mankind continuously brings forth. Your DEVOTION to God's Will is the catalyst by which Miracles are brought forth via a lifestyle of Prayer.

Everyone in your immediate social circle will be affected, and it is up to each one of them, according to God's Gift of Free Will, to decide how to make their own changes. That is not of your direct concern; your only task is to focus on how God is using your life for His Will, simply focus on radiating His Gifts through your life.

Some people around you will take notice of the positive changes you have made and of the different person you have become, but you must understand that ONLY Christ can truly observe, nourish, and preserve your spiritual GLOW.

Some who are in need of Christ's Healing will come to you to ask what your "secret" is, and some will not. It is part of your DUTY in God's Will, to discern their need and to speak or not speak appropriately to each person about your own Renewal of the mind and Healing in Christ. It benefits every being on this planet when one more individual comes to the beginning places of Christ's Love. Those who are dedicated to this process should be careful in their walk in such an evil and disconnected world. Within the Great Commission everyone is called to share his or her "personal testimony of conviction" to those they come in contact with but they are instructed to do so with Wisdom and discernment.

Do not cast your pearls before swine. Those who are soulfully and spiritually hungry are laden with their own ego-isms. The dark energies emanating from their minds can be harmful to you who are still tender in your Awakening. If you just blabber your lips, telling anyone and everyone who asks, of the amazing things God has opened your mind to, your spiritual progress becomes diminished in the eyes of these others, as well as in your own, in a process called the "draining of your Glow."

Instead, speak with respect and discernment to each individual. Some will have no understanding of what you have been experiencing. Some will totally reject it in disbelief. Some will have their own taste of Christ. Some will be as parasitic leeches to your soul and spirit, acting with interest, kindness, and helpfulness on the outside, but intending otherwise. Complete trust of another human being is a near impossibility on Earth as humanity falls very short of the Glory of God. There is only a tiny percentage of beings on this planet at any given moment who are SERIOUS about self-Renewal in Christ. Most people on Earth will continue to choose to stay dis-eased in the soul and flesh, and that is just a FACT, so you must be very careful with all people in your social circles regarding what you reveal about your spiritual progress. Many of those whom you thought of as bosom buddies will just fall away from your life as you become spiritually stronger.

If you are confused at all as to what to say or not say to another, have a conversation with God first. In the Quietude and Stillness of your Prayer Way, or talk with Christ, you will be Guided as to how to interrelate with any person you encounter.

Dedication, Diligence, Determination, and Devotion: they are amazing Rays of the Holy Spirit. Not only are they shields and swords of Christ, but they are the very nourishment of His Living Body for you and all who would Return unto Him.

Praise God!

STEP 10: PATIENCE, WHICH GIVES BIRTH TO THE FRUITS OF FAITH

Now we come back to the last crucial spirit energy, despised by every ego-ism in the mind of mankind: Patience. Patience is a virtue, indeed, and it leads to one of the Greatest Gifts that God can bestow upon a person, which is FAITH. FAITH is the belief in the things of God that are unseen, and the focus upon things hoped for, but FAITH requires the muscle of action from the one who is Gifted with FAITH. When one's daily activities are grounded in Faith, the Kingdom of God flows forth by way of that one individual spirit's life on Earth.

But what does all this really mean? What does it look like? And why is Patience such an important part of Becoming a Body of Infinity in the Christ?

All of the nine other requirements I have discussed are spiritual energies brought into activity, as is Patience. The best way to envision Patience is to visualize within your mind a Tree. Bring to mind the image of a tall Tree with a thick trunk—a giant Redwood or an Oak that has been standing for hundreds of years. Trees are the perfect embodiment of the spirit energy, Patience, as their very existence requires waiting. Waiting during the cold of Winter, waiting for the sacred rains, waiting for the constant radiation of the summer sun, the spirit of Tree always waits, in communion with the calm expectation that is inherent in Patience. Truthfully, the image I have just drawn should be enough for you to understand the importance of Patience, but I will clarify its relationship with both Faith and the Infinity of God.

When choosing to take command over the thoughts of personal will, when the timeline of the ego-ism's self-centeredness has polluted the whole of an individual's life, Patience enters. Patience is the Tree of your soul, joining forces with the knowing of your spirit that EVERYTHING that is spiritually worthy happens according to God's Time, God's Will, and by way of God's Ultimate Hand. The Tree of Patience that you are learning to imitate stills your mind and flesh, humbling you and making you more attentive to the Guidance of the Holy Spirit, not to the confines and restrictions of what your ego-isms want—and of course, ego-isms want everything NOW.

When the spirit of Patience is truly embodied, you will have evidence that your spirit is now the dominant lens through which you see all things of life on Earth. The drama of the world and of others around you will be seen for the illusory negative and dead energies that they are, and you will have no attachment to them at all. Your Patience will also invariably open the whole of your being to God's most perfect Gift of Faith.

Here is where the Kingdom of God's Infinity REALLY shines, by way of your life on Earth. Read on, and with great attention to your inhale, soak in what I am about to share. Rejoice in the following rays of Infinity

***

FAITH AS THE FIRE OF THE LIVING BODY OF CHRIST:
YOUR KEY TO BECOMING A BODY OF INFINITY

Read the following Truth as the spirit being you are; as one who now belongs fully to The ONE God Almighty Who is the Christ, Who is the Holy Spirit, and Who consumes all that you are in the Infinity of NOW.

The Fire of Christ radiates unto those who choose to open to His Presence and embody His Will in the form and Gift of Faith. Faith is His very supernatural Flame translated into the third dimension where Earth and mankind reside. His Flame of Faith is also the Muscle of His Holy Spirit by which all Goodness, All things sacred, and All Miracles are made manifest. In order for the Flame of Faith to accomplish God's Will on Earth, the spirit being who is blessed with it is required to always think and behave in such a way that the Holy Spirit is able to bestow more Flames of Faith to that person. A spirit being such as this desires more radiance from God, always, and eventually CHOOSES to live in communion with Him—To BECOME the COMMUNION in CHRIST. This means that the whole of the mind is in alignment with Christ's Mind, and the body is now subject to the Healing Rays of Christ, so that it can truly be physiologically altered towards conditions of Good or perfect health, with the Heart alighting with the Fire of God's Will.

Faith is embodied in the symbol of Infinity, and can be understood as such. When one is Gifted with Faith, which only comes from God, one is nourished in such a way that one chooses to change EVERYTHING about one's former ways to the WAY of belonging to God alone. This is putting the Flame of Faith into action, which then leads to God's Gifting of more Faith. Where there is more Faith there is more manifestation of God's Will. Where God's Will is manifested, there is the Kingdom of Heaven. It is a never ending and continuous stream of the Flame put into action as more Faith is received, and put into action as more Faith received, and on and on, for the benefit of all mankind. BREATHE THIS.

In this there is no longer any "personal life" on. There is only the perfection of knowing yourself as the unique spirit being you are, armed and poised in Faithful Action of the Holy Spirit. You will encounter many evils of this world, burning through them with focused concentration of Truth. By way of your influence upon them all those who are chosen by God will come to reject evil and remember truly who they are and why they are on Earth.

When The Lord Jesus Christ comes again, you will be shown that you have done your part by choosing to cleanse yourself—to be Healed in all ways—all the while radiating the very Will of God. And most amazingly of all, you will know that you have become a body of His Infinity, even while in human form on Earth. What Miracles you will witness! But let those Miracles be seen and acknowledged by you in this very moment.

Make today the First Day in your perfect Communion in Creator! Live truly for this moment, day in and day out, when He comes to take you fully. This joyous living in Christ will keep you fortified in the stream of His Plan, with his Mind saturating your own, His Heart pulsing through your own, His Body captivating your every cell. All this pouring forth without ceasing as He watches what the world would choose.

In this moment you see how you are a part of the realm of God's Miraculous Body of Infinity! You, in this body and in this lifetime, now have the keys to Breathing the Kingdom of God as you would Receive. It is your responsibility to walk into these Rays, to grow ever stronger, and to radiate them constantly while you are in this world. The Will of God Breathes you in this Way.

I am a Voice of Christ's Healing so blessedly inhaling and Singing unto the furthest reaches of God's Infinity, in devotional Prayer, in order that you may come to embody the Fire Light of our Holy Lord God Almighty—NOW.

***

THE PRACTICAL APPLICATION OF HEALING PRINCIPLES

The journey of Healing that I have chosen is, at its supernatural core, the Fire of God Almighty's Spirit translated into this third dimension. I have repeated throughout this book that God's Will, God's Hand, God's Unfathomable Mind and God's Heart are the ONLY means by which a person is able to Receive Healing and Wholeness.

It is also Truth that not all spirit beings are endowed with the same gifts of the Holy Spirit. Faith, Knowledge, Wisdom, Healing, working of Miracles, Prophecy, discerning of spirits, gift of tongues, interpretation of tongues are the nine gifts described in the Holy Bible, but they are not the full extent of them.

A person who comes to live in communion with and for God alone, is blessed uniquely, and is given the Grace to discover what Gifts are to be used through his or her life on Earth. This is a process that is not bound by time, but for human beings it requires warrior-like patience, humility, and focus for the Gifts to emerge and grow strong in one's life.

You will never know yourself as a spirit being of God's Design if you allow your ego to speak and breathe as your dominant voice.

But...

You can and should take action in accordance to God's Will as Guided by the Holy Spirit in response to sincere Prayer. Your choices, within the Healing that God Wills forth for YOU, will be utterly unique, perfect, and effective.

This appendix is a summary of my own Healing techniques and practices, including exercise and nutrition. I share it here to give you a lens of perspective that will inspire you to unite with God's own Plan for your Healing and Wholeness, moment by moment.

Whereas the 10 Requirements of Becoming a Body of Infinity listed earlier in this book are of a spiritual nature, the following list describes the physical practices that I have chosen to incorporate within the Healing along the way. They are indeed a part of the HUM.

This list is not necessarily meant to be followed to the letter, but is intended as a guide to help you find what works best for you. To that end, I have explained how each practice was of benefit to myself, and have made suggestions as to their implementation. Many of the listings are self-explanatory. Some things that you are guided to activate in your life will remain constant for the rest of your body's time on Earth, other practices may only be engaged for six months, a few weeks, perhaps only for a day, depending on your needs

All that is required is your commitment, your ability to listen and learn, and your humility in the process of Healing as it unfolds, as it most certainly will.

The following information is shared as a Living Prayer that your soul and flesh will inhale, in each and every moment, the Healing Light that is your spirit's birthright in God Almighty.

ELISE'S LIST OF HEALING PRACTICES

1. IMMERSE YOURSELF IN NATURE:
   a. Plant and tend a garden. Become familiar with and taste the produce of the Garden—that includes the "weeds" as well as the cultivated crops and flowers, including the whole of Dandelion, Violets, Burdock, grasses, White and Red Clover flowers, Chickweed, etc., taking care to first ascertain their edibility.
   b. Hike a trail, taking the time to see the details of your surroundings.
   c. Study the Plant and Animal Kingdoms.
   d. Adopt an animal Companion and care for all Animals that come under your domain.
   e. Walk barefoot in Nature whenever possible.
   f. Spend time in the sunshine.

2. EAT PURELY
   a. Eat abundantly of green vegetables, fruits, beans, nuts, and the meat of lovingly raised animals.
   b. Drink ample quantities of kombucha and herbal teas such as Nettles, Red Raspberry, Oatstraw, Red Clover, Ginger, or Dandelion roots and leaves.
   c. Drink generous amounts of pure Water.

These herbs helped to raise my blood iron levels while on the Healing path from Anorexia, and nourished me during both pregnancies as well. They all continue to cleanse and fortify my organs and blood. While their physiological effects are amazing, their impact as individual spirit beings is even more profound. They continue to reveal secrets to me, even after all these years of partaking of them.

I drink on average a gallon of purified Water each day, thanks to our reverse osmosis filtration system. I started consuming this amount during my pregnancies, but have continued ever since. (Don't worry, your kidneys and bladder will adjust, and in a few weeks, you will be more comfortable with this volume, if you know what I mean.)

3. FAST SELECTIVELY

From time to time choose one type of nut, vegetable, or fruit to eat for one whole day as a form of toxic cleansing and nutritional awareness. Be cautious in this and seek proper guidance as needed. As one begins to eat reasonably and according to Wholeness, the body will begin to clear out the toxins. For example, once a month, I would eat just kale for one day, the next month it would be just pecans, etc., so that I could observe how my flesh responded to that particular food's frequency and spirit. This is a great way to learn about and to commune with the spirit beings of food as well as with the Earth and Sun. Selective Food Fasting will also help you to rid your flesh and mind of dangerous vices that are contrary to the health of your spirit being. As my body was cleansed and nourished, I came to Remember what the BODY of Christ really is: the holiness of pure Air, Water, Food, and the WORD of the Living God.

4. MEDITATE AND PRAY REGULARLY:

Make space each morning, afternoon, and evening to give your WHOLE being to God alone. For nearly 10 years it was my practice to sit in meditation and prayer for an hour in the morning, a half-hour at lunch, and another hour at bedtime. This has changed over the years, as meditation and Prayer have come to interfuse every aspect of my life, no matter where I am or what I am doing. A practice of sitting meditation should involve a space of time where attention is given to the Breath alone. Prayer however, is TALKING with God in privacy. Prayer can take many forms. It can be expressed as art, music or literature, or it can simply be internal conversations with God. There are NO rules about Prayer except to say that true Prayer is between God and you alone.

5. Practice Yoga and Exercise:

I have always loved to feel the cleansing physiological flush brought on by swimming, running, fast-paced walking, climbing trees, dance, or isometric exercises, finding in exercise a form of perfect Prayer and a different kind of meditation. The mind is not so active during aerobic exercise, and the body is breathing hard with necessary focus on breath. I precede each workout with intentional Prayer to bring forth a specific energy or for the needs of specific people, Receiving wondrous and encouraging messages and responses during the workout.

I love honoring Creator and all Life in this way, embodying Gratitude and Healing through sweat, but my first and preferred practice for the care of the flesh is YOGA.

The Yoga I practice has nothing to do with Hinduism or any religious system. It is rather, a practical set of techniques designed to help human beings develop an awareness of their deepest nature. Postural Yoga, or asanas, are forms of Prayer that your body is disciplined to imitate. When you practice Yoga asanas your body opens to receive the outpouring of God's Fire. Your breath becomes the medium by which the Holy Spirit reaches and teaches you on the path to becoming a body of Infinity. Unlike aerobic exercise, you do not sweat, but your breath deepens, allowing you to focus on God and on your place within Creator's Life.

As I focused on the stretching of my flesh and on the movement of my Breath, I learned where the sin and lies in my life had been stuffed away. Each and every posture carried God's Rays of Healing. My blood and synovial fluids began to wash through, bringing nourishment to starved bones, and comfort to damaged joints. With complete Faith and dutiful practice, those areas of strife have all been lifted, corrected, and Healed of the filth once lodged in them.The revelations never end. Yoga constantly beckons the student to go deeper in Breath, Higher in Love of God, bringing forth exquisite manifestations of Healing unique for each person. Yoga is a Gift from God.

6. MAKE WORK IN ALL ITS FORMS AN ACT OF DEVOTION TO GOD:

I have worked in many places doing all kinds of mundane manual labor. I have also been graced to be a group coordinator, teacher of Spanish and music, doula and midwife, a patient representative in an Orthopedic Institute, Associate Vice-President of the Bliss-Parsons Institute, a writer, singer, and traveling minister of Christ's Healing. In each and every one of these positions, I have always seen it as my duty to radiate Christ. Even when I was flipping burgers at White Castle, sweating for nine hours non-stop, I knew that I was bringing forth nourishment from God. Sure, I had many moments of "I really do not want to be here," but I have always been able to silence the voices of selfishness and self-centered ego-isms in remembrance of the billions of people of this world who suffer so terribly in their daily quest to simply remain alive.

To choose to have a heart, which feels the plight of others, and to work hard in Prayer that the radiance of God's Love might reach them, is sublime! I have always remembered the Sacrifice of Christ and His Work that can never be imitated or equated. It is this last thought that has always been enough to give me the strength to laugh at any attempt by ego-isms to distract me from TRUTH. I place myself in God's Heart in EVERYTHING I do, no matter where I am.

7. GET RIGHT WITH GOD BY GETTING RID OF EVIL ENERGY IN RELATIONSHIPS:

None of the people in my former social circles nourished my Awakening and Return to the Truth of God, so I dropped ALL of them. This was a drastic move on my part, as I had been a social butterfly in the garden of home birthing, a doula and midwife, organizing blessing ways and potlucks, and any other excuse to bring together groups of mothers and babies frequently.

It is not easy in this world to surround yourself with quiet Prayer warriors who cherish God above and beyond all else, and I am certainly not emanating spiritual elitism in saying that this is the only type of friendship a person should have. All people on this planet are addicted to ego-isms to various degrees, and it must be carefully calculated how much of another's worldly ways one wants to expose one's tender soul to. Ask yourself the question: What do I enjoy about this friendship? What do I give to this person and what do I receive from this relationship? Does this person boost up God's Love in his or her own life? Am I loving God more by way of this friendship? If your answers resonate positively in your heart and mind, then by all means, maintain that relationship. If your answers bring forth doubt or negativity in any fashion, then something is off balance and you are not serving that person's spiritual growth or your own. Keep in mind at all times that intimate and social relationships have great power to either build up or break down a person in this life.

8. Make God Your Everything

My spiritual return to knowing that God is All occurred not as a moment in time, but interwoven throughout the story of my Healing. The time it took for me to Remember my spiritual covenant to God's Work for this world was relatively short as reckoned on Earth, but in those years of entrenched suffering, it seemed like forever. No human marriage, no diet, no church, no job, no worldly place of prestige, no person or thing will bring Indomitable Love, Wholeness and Healing to you.

The past is truly and completely obliterated in the Truth of Jesus the Christ. Why waste another moment looking for assistance with things that are of no spiritual value? Here's the key: time is irrelevant when you make God your EVERYTHING. Other worthy human relationships will appear if they serve His Purpose. In the infinity of NOW Healing becomes a Reality, and God's Will becomes your heart's passion. Time exists only here on Earth, and you have to make every moment come alive if you truly intend to embark upon the path to Becoming a Body of Infinity.

***

ELISE'S PHOTO ALBUM

Elise conversing with the Flowers of Annica in the Sacred Heart Garden

God's Altar of Annica
It is in front of this altar that many Songs are first created and weekly editions of Voice of Christ's Healing are recorded.

About 1969

Elise's biological parents

Dr. Pacelli Escondo Brion (Lilli to his Family)

Newborn Elise held by her maternal grandmother, Elsie. Writing on photo is from Pacelli's hand and reads "Nene at 20 days old 01/25/77."

4-year-old Elise, foretelling her future as a writer.

Joyful soul and spirit of Elise at 4 and 5 years old.

Elise at 4 years old. Outdoors at one of the homes of her childhood.

1981
Elise, her older sister, and their grandmother, Elsie.

With maternal grandparents, Tom & Elsie, at their home in Erlanger, Kentucky, USA

Self-portrait with Milkshake (the Cat)
Chalk drawing done at age 6 framed and hanging on wall of one of 2 childhood homes.

First Communion - 7 years old
(Notice her mother in the doorway.)

Beloved Tree Friend, Scylla
A place of many hours of Childhood Prayers. After all these years, Scylla still stands and is sought often as a place of quiet refuge.

Older sister, Elise (11 years old), and Grandma Elsie in Kentucky

At age 17, with Persimmon, the one-eyed shitza-cocka-poo

At age 22, one month before the heart attack on the trail

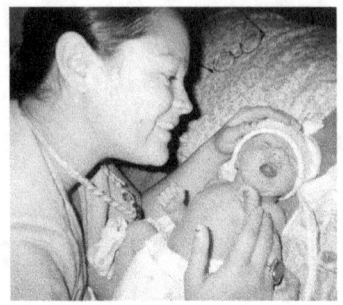

At age 24, with newborn son. Birthed at home in water after 42 hour labor.

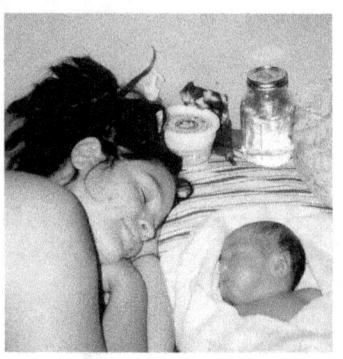

At age 27, with newborn daughter. Same home, same bathtub, shorter labor.

After play with Children.
Winter art in the Snow of Annica

ABOUT THE AUTHOR

Elise R. Brion knows she is not of this world. Her purpose and mission is to embody and radiate the Healing Will of God to mankind. It is to that end that she dedicates her original music, published books, and ministry, *Voice of Christ's Healing*.

Having Testified and performed for over 13 years at schools, hospitals, prisons, hospices, psychiatric wards, churches and more, Ms. Brion has Witnessed to thousands. Her life demonstrates how God's timeless Truth of Healing goes far beyond the physical realms. She teaches how that Healing may be achieved, and that Infinity is to be entered into not after death, but NOW.

Find the *Voice of Christ's Healing* videos on YouTube, her albums on cdBaby.com, and Ms. Brion on Facebook.

www.ingramcontent.com/pod-product-compliance
Lightning Source LLC
Chambersburg PA
CBHW071904290426
44110CB00013B/1276